Publisher's Cataloging-in Publication
(Provided by Quality Books, Inc.)

Hunting, William
    The art of horse-shoeing: a manual for farriers / by
William Hunting.
      p. cm.—(The farrier classics; no. 1)
      Includes index.
      Reprint of 1895 title.
      "With nearly one hundred illustrations."
      ISBN: 0-944079-28-8

    1. Horseshoeing—Handbooks, manuals, etc. I. Title.

SF907.H86 1998   682'.1
                               QBI98-884

Cover Art By Gene Matras

International Standard Book Number: 0-944079-28-8

Published by Lessiter Media,
P.O. Box 624, Brookfield, WI 53008-0624.
For additional copies or information on other
Lessiter Media books or product, write to the above address.
Telephone: (800) 645-8455 or (262) 782-4480.
Fax: (262) 782-1252. E-Mail: info@americanfarriers.com
Manufactured In The United States of America

THE
ART OF HORSE-SHOEING
A Manual for Farriers,

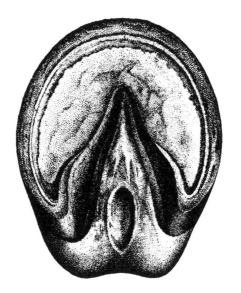

BY

WILLIAM HUNTING, F.R.C.V.S.

Editor of The Veterinary Record.
Veterinary Inspector for Westminster and Chelsea.
Consulting Veterinary Surgeon to the London Road-Car Company.
Member of the Committee for National Registration of Farriers.

With nearly one hundred Illustrations.

London :

H. & W. BROWN, 20 FULHAM ROAD, S.W.

1895.

A VALUABLE
SHOEING REFERENCE

Recognized among equine historians as one of the top dozen books of all time on horseshoeing techniques, William Hunting's "The Art Of Horse-Shoeing: A Manual For Farriers" was originally published in Great Britain in 1895.

Many highly practical trimming and shoeing ideas, philosophies and techniques which Hunting describes in his book are based on the British veterinarian's experiences during the late 1800s and are still essential to good shoeing. More than 100 years later, many farriers are still making extensive use of the many valuable shoeing techniques described in this book.

In "On The Horse's Foot, Shoes And Shoeing: The Bibliographic Record," author Henry Heymering called this book "An excellent guide to horseshoeing—

clear, concise and accurate. "For valuable insights as to the tremendous hoof-care reference value of this book, be sure to check out William Hunting's preface, written in 1895.

With reprinting of this 1895 book, *American Farriers Journal* is proud to launch "The Farrier Classics" series of hoof-care books.

Our goal is to find out-of-print historical shoeing and hoof-care reference books that are still highly valuable to shoers, veterinarians, researchers, trainers and owners keenly interested in learning more about all aspects of equine foot care.

Through "The Farrier Classics," we'll share the very best time-honored techniques, ideas, tips and reference materials regarding equine hoof care which have stood the test of time.

—FRANK LESSITER
EDITOR/PUBLISHER
AMERICAN FARRIERS JOURNAL

CONTENTS.

PREFACE.

This little book is written for three classes of readers—for horse-owners who may interest themselves in the subject, for farriers who are open to conviction, and for veterinary students who have to be examined.

The method pursued has been, to first describe the form and action of the foot, next the preparation of the foot for shoeing. Then the form of a shoe is treated of and the details to be observed in making it. The selection of shoes for varieties of feet or for special kinds of work follows, and afterwards the fitting and nailing-on are considered. Other chapters are devoted to " roughing," shoeing defective feet, accidents, the use of leathers and pads.

Throughout an endeavour has been made to be as simple and clear as possible in expression, to lay down correct general principles and to point out the technical details which are essential to good shoeing. On all these points authorities are not agreed, and I trust those who differ from me will pardon any too dogmatic expressions of opinion in these pages.

The illustrations will be of assistance in making clear the text. Some of these are copied from books, some are drawn from models or preparations, and some are diagramatic. The books I am indebted to are, " Anatomy of the Domestic Animals," by Gamgee and Laws; " On the Horse's Foot," by Bracy Clark; Bouley's " Atlas of the Foot," and Goyau's " Maréchalerie."

WILLIAM HUNTING.

16 Trafalgar Square,
London, S.W.

THE

ART OF HORSE-SHOEING

A MANUAL FOR FARRIERS.

CHAPTER I.

Farriery is the art of shoeing horses, and can only be properly learned by a long practical experience in the shoeing-forge. If the foot of the horse were not a living object perhaps the training obtained in the forge would be all that was necessary for efficient workmanship   As, however, the hoof is constantly growing it is constantly changing its form. The duty of a farrier therefore is not merely to fix a shoe upon the hoof but to reduce the hoof to proper proportions before doing so.   Now as hoof is only the outer covering of a complex and sensitive foot, damage to the exterior surface may injure the structures within.   Injury does frequently result, and not always from carelessness.   Perhaps as much injury follows careful work, based upon wrong principles, as slovenly work carried out in perfect ignorance of any principle. The injury to feet resulting from shoeing may not be apparent at once.   It may be, and often is, of a slow and gradual nature, and not credited to its true cause until the horse is rendered an incurable cripple.

It seems evident then that to do justice to a horse a farrier should not only possess manipulative skill, but should have a correct idea of the structures and functions of the foot, as well as a thorough knowledge of the form and variations of the hoof.

Few persons appreciate the importance of horse-shoeing, whilst a small number tell us it is unnecessary.   Here and there an enthusiast has the courage of his convictions and is able, for a time, to exhibit animals doing work without shoes. In some countries horses are regularly ridden with no addition to their natural hoof, but in such places the surface over which the animals travel is grass land. In all civilised countries where good roads exist shoeing is practised. The gentleman with a fad who occasionally appears in England with unshod horses at work is an unconscious impostor. He sets his little experience against the common sense and universal practice of others. No man of business would pay for shoeing if he could do without it. The " shoeless" experiment has been tried over and over again, but always with the same result—a return to shoeing. In dry weather the hoof becomes hard, and it is wonderful how much wear it will then stand on the hardest of roads. In wet weather the hoof becomes soft, and then the friction on hard roads soon prohibits work without shoes. If work be persisted in, under such circumstances, the hoof rapidly wears away and lameness results. Persons trying to prove a pre-conceived theory meet this difficulty by resting the horse until the horn grows, but business men who keep horses for work in all weathers can afford no such luxury. Shoeing has been called " a necessary evil." The phrase is a misuse of words, for there is no necessary evil about it. Of course it is no more free from accident than other operations, but its evils are fairly described as accidents, whilst its benefits are fully apparent. Without shoes horses at work would be more often lame than with them ; without shoes horses could not do half the work they do with them, and so we need not further discuss the necessity of shoeing.

The value of horse-shoeing depends upon the manner in which it is done. Very seldom does the owner of horses appreciate the quality of the work. As a rule the price charged, or the distance from the forge to the stable, regulates the choice of a farrier. Not having any pecuniary interest in the trade, I may say that such matters should not be allowed to decide between one farrier and another. A bad workman may do an injury at one shoeing which will cost the owner of the horse more than would pay ten times over the difference between his charges and the higher prices of a better man.

Many years ago I knew a firm who changed their farrier and system of shoeing for a cheaper plan. The cost for shoeing alone fell very considerably, but the cost of horse-flesh rose in one year more than £100. The old saw—" that for want of a nail the shoe was lost, for want of a shoe the horse was lost, and for want of a horse the man was lost," has been illustrated times without number. Few persons, however, are aware of the terrible consequences which have more than once attended neglect in the shoeing of horses. Napoleon's retreat from Moscow depended for most of its hardships and horrors upon the simple fact that his horses were not shod properly for travelling on snow and ice. The horses could not keep their feet, and were unable to drag the guns and waggons, which had to be abandoned. During the Franco-Prussian war, Bourbaki's retreat became a confused rout from a similar cause. In civil life no winter passes without injury and death to hundreds of horses from the same neglect. These are instances that anyone can see; but heavy losses due to bad shoeing are constant from other or less evident evils—from the adoption of wrong methods and the practice of erroneous theories.

The farrier has not been fairly treated by the public. His practical knowledge has been ignored, he has been instructed by amateurs in all sorts of theories, and coerced into carrying out practices for the untoward results of which he has been blamed. The natural consequence of all this has been that the art of farriery degenerated, and the farrier was forced into a position destructive to the self-respect of any craftsman. In no other trade do persons entirely ignorant of the business presume to direct and dictate as to how the work should be done. No one presumes to instruct the watch-maker or bell-hanger as to the details of his craft, but the farrier has been compelled to take his instructions from all sorts and conditions of men.

Only in recent years has the man who shoes horses been allowed to know something of his calling. Various causes have acted in putting an end to the state of discord, and the trade is now entering upon a brighter time. The Worshipful Company of Farriers —one of those ancient City Guilds which had survived their original vocation and usefulness—has wakened up, and is striving to resume it proper function as the head and director of the trade over which it ought to preside. Agricultural Societies have also taken the matter up, and fostered a healthy emulation amongst farriers by instituting practical competitions at their shows. Veterinary Surgeons have devoted considerable research to the elucidation of the anatomy and physiology of the foot, and many old errors have been corrected. School Boards have made the present generation of farriers able and willing to supplement their practice by a study of principles. We have, in fact, arrived at a time when everyone interested seems inclined to recognise the importance of the art and its technical difficulties, and when no one has a brand new infallible discovery which alone can save the horse and guide the farrier.

My object in writing is not to suggest anything new but to point out the general principles upon which the art is based, and to indicate those details which are essential to success, and those which are to be avoided if soundness and duration of service are recognised as true economy in a stud of horses.

CHAPTER II.

THE FORM AND ACTION OF THE FOOT.

The foot of a horse consists of a variety of living structures, differing in form and texture, and enclosed in a horny covering called the hoof. Although the farrier's work is applied only to the hoof it is necessary that he should know something of the whole foot, because it is but too easy to injure the structures within by alterations of the horny covering without.

The simplest way to understand the foot is to study separately the different parts, and to apply that knowledge in obtaining a general idea of the relations of all the parts to each other. There is not then much difficulty in appreciating the functions of each part, and the uses and action of the whole organ.

THE HOOF.

Everyone is familiar with the general appearance of the hoof. It is not a regular geometrical figure. Each of the four feet of the horse shows some peculiarity in form, by which a farrier can at once identify a fore from a hind or a left from a right.

The fore feet should be similar in size and shape. Disease may be suspected when any marked difference exists. But a healthy hoof which has been broken, or much rasped, does not retain its proper form and may thus confuse a novice.

The hind feet should be proportionate in size to the fore, and then it is not of much practical consequence whether the whole are large or small.

The front feet are rounder and less pointed at the toe than the hind; they are also more sloping in front. The two fore feet and the two hind should be in pairs. The right and left feet are distinguished from each other by the inner side being more upright or, if examined on the under surface, by the outer border being more prominent.

Although to a casual observer the hoof appears as one continuous horny structure, it may easily be separated into three distinct parts by prolonged soaking in water. The division takes place so as to leave the sole, frog, and wall separate portions. These may now be considered.

10

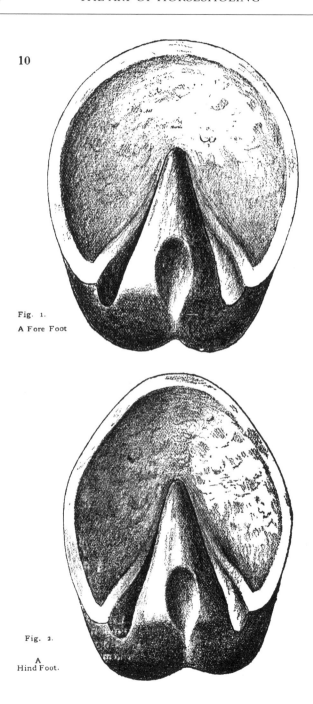

Fig. 1.
A Fore Foot

Fig. 2.

A
Hind Foot.

The **Wall** is that portion of the hoof seen whilst the foot rests upon the ground. It covers the front and sides of the foot. It extends from the coronet downwards and slightly outwards so that its lower circumference is greater than its upper. The front portion shows its greatest height and obliquity, diminishing in these respects as it passes backwards. At the heels the wall is turned in upon itself, and passes forward towards the centre of the foot until it becomes lost in the structure of the sole. These turned-in portions of the wall are called *the bars*, and serve two purposes ; they increase the bearing surface of the wall, and by embracing a part of the sole on each side, they afford an increased solidity to the union of the wall with the rest of the hoof.

If we detach the wall its inner surface is seen to consist of a number of thin horny projections running parallel to each other from above downwards and forwards. These are called the horny laminæ. They number from five to six hundred and correspond to similar processess on the sensitive foot. (Fig. 3).

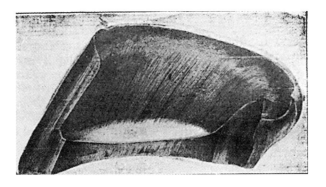

Fig. 3.—Half of a Hoof, showing the inside.

Round the upper circumference on the inside of the **wall** is a depression or groove presenting innumerable small pits or openings. This corresponds to a part of the sensitive foot called the coronary band, which will be noticed again.

A section of wall enables us to see variations in its thickness. (Fig. 4). It is thickest at the toe, becoming gradually thinner towards the heels ; thus affording strength and solidity to resist wear at one part, as well as pliancy at another to ward off concussion.

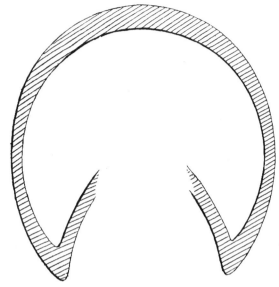

Fig. 4.—Transverse Section of Wall showing variation in thickness.

The structure of the wall is fibrous—the fibres running parallel to each other, and with the same obliquity as that presented by the front of the wall. Although the wall varies in thickness from before backwards, it does not from above downwards. It maintains the same thickness from the coronet to its lower circumference.

The layers of the wall are hardest externally, becoming softer as they approach the inner surface—a condition due to the outer layers being exposed to friction and evaporation. This is a simple and valuable provision of nature which should not be interfered with. The hard outer layer is best adapted to withstand wear, and its density protects the deeper layers from evaporation. This maintains the whole wall at the degree of softness and toughness which best preserves elasticity and strength of horn.

The Sole is that division of the hoof which forms the floor of the foot. It is situated within the lower border of the wall, and is slightly arched so that on a hard level surface its central part takes no bearing. (Fig. 5.) Posteriorly the sole is divided by a triangular space into which the frog fits, and thus its continuation to the heels consists of two angular portions embraced between the bars and the wall.

The unmutilated sole is throughout of nearly equal thickness, but a slight excess round the circumference gives firmer attachment to the wall.

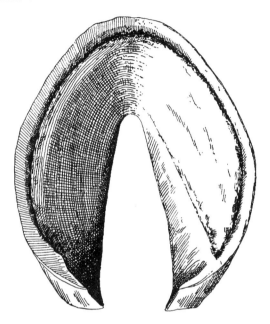

Fig. 5.—The Sole with Frog removed.

The inner surface presents a finely pitted appearance which is most marked at the toe and round its border. The part immediately related to the frog shows few pits, and we shall find that the whole surface corresponds to the sensitive parts to which it is attached.

The structure of the sole is, like the wall, fibrous; but the fibres are smaller. They run downwards and forwards in the same direction as those of the wall. The outer layers are the hardest and protect the deeper from injury.

The Frog is the smallest division of the hoof, and is a triangular shaped body filling up the space left between the bars. (Fig. 6). Its broad base is rounded and prominent, and is continued laterally by a thin layer which binds together the heels and envelopes the back of the foot. This thin layer is continuous with a horny band extending round the upper part of the wall at its junction with the hair, and sometimes prolonged downwards on the surface of the wall.

(Fig. 7). It appears to be a continuation of the outer layer of the skin, analogous to the free border of skin at the root of the human nail. (Fig 8). It serves the useful purpose of covering and protecting the young horn of the wall at its source of growth.

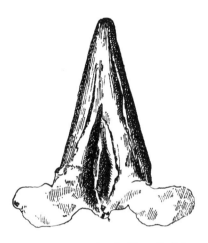

Fig. 6.   The Frog, detached from the Sole.

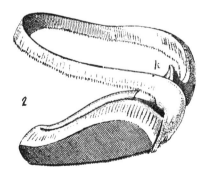

Fig. 7. –The Frog and frog-band.

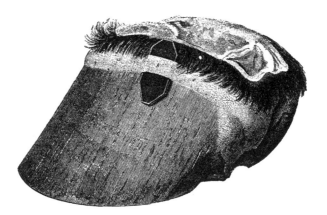

Fig. 8.—The frog band detached from wall by a small wedge.

The point of the frog, much the harder part, extends forward to the centre of the sole. Though situated between the bars the frog is only attached to their upper border—the sides remaining free and separate. Thus on each side is formed a deep fissure which permits the frog to expand laterally when compressed, without such force being continued to the sides of the foot. The frog is elastic, and when pressed upon must expand slightly If these spaces between frog and bars did not exist, the foot would be injured when the frog was compressed by the weight of the horse—either the sensitive parts within would be bruised or the heels would be forced apart.

The centre of the frog presents a depression or "cleft" caused by the doubling in of the horn. Few shod feet exhibit it of natural appearance, and the term cleft, by implying a narrow deep fissure, keeps up the false notion. The cleft should be shallow and rounded. It serves two purposes—it increases the mobility of the frog, and by breaking the regularity of surface affords a secure foot-hold on level ground.

The prominence of the frog might lead a superficial observer to consider it a thick solid mass ; and I believe this mistake is the cause of its too frequent mutilation. It is merely a layer of horn following the outline of the structures within, which are similarly prominent and irregular in surface. (Figs. 9 and 10). The diagrams show a section through the point and through the cleft of the frog.

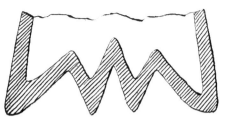

Fig. 9.—Section of Foot at cleft.

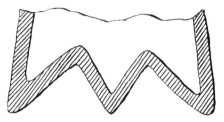

Fig. 10.—Section at point.

The frog is fibrous, though not to such a marked degree as the other portions of the hoof Its chief qualities are elasticity and toughness.

THE SECRETING STRUCTURES.

If we macerate a dead foot in water for a week or two, the hoof may be removed entire without injuring the tissues within. In this way the sensitive foot or " quick " is exposed to view, and presents an exact counterpart of the inside of the hoof. The sensitive foot consists of a layer of fibrous tissue stretched over the bones and other structures which form the centre of the foot It is plentifully supplied with blood-vessels and nerves necessary to its double function as the source of horn growth and as the tactile organ of the foot. Horn is, of course, not sensitive, although the slightest touch on a horse's hoof is recognised by the animal, and this feeling is due to the impression made upon the sensitive foot. In the living horse any injury to the " quick " causes the greatest pain, and although this sensitiveness is a serious disadvantage in disease it is a most valuable provision in health, enabling the horse, even through a thick layer of horn, to recognise the quality of the surface upon which he may be standing or moving It is this sense of touch—this tactile function—which demands that the sensitive foot should be so bountifully supplied with nerves.

Every farrier knows how profusely blood flows from any wound of the "quick"—evidence that the part is well supplied with blood-vessels. This full supply of blood is not merely for the ordinary waste and repair which takes place in every tissue; it is to meet a special demand—to supply the material for the production of horn. The sensitive foot is the secreting structure of the hoof, and the source of the constant growth and reproduction of horn It corresponds with great exactness to the inside of the hoof, and as we have described the hoof in sections it may be convenient to follow that course with this structure, and to describe the *sensitive frog*, the *sensitive sole*, and the *sensitive laminæ*. We shall begin with the last.

The Sensitive Laminæ. Corresponding to the horny leaves on the inside of the wall, the sensitive foot presents an arrangement of minute parallel folds which are called the sensitive laminæ. (Fig. 11). Between these the horny laminæ rest, so that there is a kind of interleaved attachment which affords the very firmest connection between the wall and the sensitive foot. If the laminæ be laid bare in a living horse by removal of the wall, it is found that they have the power to secrete a kind of horn, not a hard fibrous horn like that of the wall, but a softer variety This function is not very active in health or we should find that the lower edge of the wall was thicker than the upper; but it exists, and is very evident in some cases of disease.

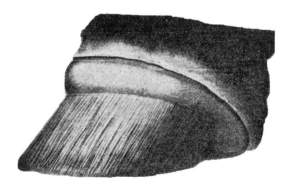

Fig. 11.—Foot with hoof removed showing at the upper part the Coronary band, and below the Sensitive Laminæ.

In laminitis the wall at the toe is often pushed forward out of position by a horny mass formed by the laminæ, and so we have the deformity of an excessive length of toe.   In some cases of long continued sandcrack the irritation of the laminæ causes excessive secretion, and a horn tumour results. The sensitive laminæ, then, fulfil two functions ; they offer a firm connecting medium for the wall, and they secrete horn.   By the cruel experiment of removing the horny sole and frog of a living horse and then forcing him to stand on the maimed foot on a level surface, it has been shown that the laminæ are capable of alone supporting the weight of the animal.   It has been argued from this that the laminæ always support the weight, and that the horse's foot may be described as being slung by the connecting laminæ.   This is not true.   The frog and sole help to support weight, and the hoof acts as one continuous whole, each part taking its direct and proportionate share of the weight placed upon the foot.   The sensitive laminæ are not elastic, they are unyielding, and, therefore, allow no downward yielding which would impose excessive pressure on the sole.

The Coronary Band. (See Fig. 11). The sensitive laminæ do not cover the whole of the upright portions of the sensitive foot.   There is between their upper extremity and the line which separates the skin from the sensitive foot, a convex band which runs round the upper border of the foot, and is turned downwards and inwards at the heels. This is called the coronary band, and corresponds to the groove which we noticed on the inner side of the upper border of the wall.   On its surface are innumerable small pro-jections or papillæ which, in the living animal, fit into the openings on the groove of the wall.   From each of these papillæ grows a horn fibre, and from the surface be-tween them is formed a softer horny matter—the two pro-ducts forming together the substance of the wall.   The coronary band is, then, an important structure, being the source from whence the wall is produced.   Upon the healthy condition of this band depends the soundness of the wall, and any interference with its integrity must lead to defects or deformities in the wall.

The Sensitive Sole (Fig. 12) is that portion of the " quick " to which the sole is attached. Its surface is covered with papillæ, like those on the coronary band but much smaller, giving an appearance somewhat like the pile of velvet.   **From**

these the horn fibres of the sole are formed, and a firm means of connection is afforded for the floor of the hoof.

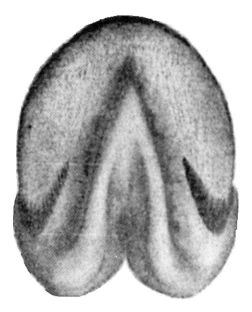

Fig. 12.—Under Surface of Foot showing Sensitive Frog and Sole.

The Sensitive Frog in structure resembles the sensitive sole, but its papillæ are very much smaller, and the surface therefore is smoother.   The irregular prominent surface of the frog, with its cleft and the space at each side of it, is exactly reproduced on the sensitive frog, as might be expected, for the one is moulded on the other. There is one difference between the sensitive frog and the other portions of the sensitive foot which I may here mention.   It is not attached to the bones of the foot except by its point, but is situated behind the bone, and has as a basis a mass of soft tissue which forms an important cushion or pad, to be referred to later.

GROWTH OF HOOF.

Like every other part of an animal body, the hoof is constantly changing.   Wear and tear cause waste of the horn, which is replenished by growth.   When wear exceeds growth the foot becomes denuded of horn, and lameness results. When growth exceeds wear the hoof becomes disproportionately long, and some parts suffer by the overgrowth of others—for instance, whenever the heels are unduly high the frog becomes small and weak. In a state of nature the horse's foot keeps itself of proportionate form. On hard ground the hoof is worn away as quickly as it grows. On soft ground it may, for a time, become overgrown, but this is rectified by the soft horn becoming fractured and broken off. In enclosed cultivated grounds the movements of the horse, even on grass land, are too limited to ensure a proportionate form of hoof. When horses are turned out without shoes the feet should not be left to take care of themselves, unless the pasture is of large area and the time at grass extends for several months.

In a hoof which is overgrown—and all shod feet become overgrown in four or five weeks—there is apparently a greater excess of horn at the toe than elsewhere This is due to the oblique direction of the wall at the toe, and to the fact that the horn fibres of the hoof do not grow down vertically, but obliquely forward. When the natural wear of the hoof is prevented, the effect of growth is to lengthen the toe and carry forward the bearing surface of the foot. Now this bearing surface has a proper relative position to the limb above it. Therefore a disproportionate foot must injuriously affect both the action and position of the whole limb.

The rate at which the wall grows varies greatly in different horses, and is affected by external conditions The good average wall grows nearly one inch in three months, and the whole hoof is replaced in from ten to fifteen months. The hoof grows more rapidly when a horse is actively exercised than when he is confined in a box. Febrile diseases check growth, and irregularities of the system cause the formation of ridges in the horn, each one commencing at the coronet and being carried down with the growing horn until the hoof is marked by a series of rings running transversely and parallel to each other. These rings are of themselves no detriment to a horse, but they mark irregularities of growth which may have been due to illness or lameness

The growth of horn on a shod foot is affected by the bearing it takes. When a part of the wall takes no bearing on the shoe it grows quicker than that which does. We see this when a shoe is so fitted that the heels take no direct pressure on the shoe, also when a portion of wall is broken at the quarters, and again when, for any reason, a portion of the edge of the wall has been rasped away to prevent bearing upon some special spot. In all these cases, after the shoe has been worn a month, it will be found that the horn has grown more rapidly at the part where bearing did not take place, and, when the shoe is removed, the horn which was relieved of pressure is found to have been in apposition with the shoe.

The growth of horn cannot be accelerated by any application to its surface. If we desire to hasten growth of the wall we can do so by stimulating the part from which it is produced, *i.e.*, the coronary band. A mild blister to the coronet causes considerable increase in the rapidity of growth, but no ointments applied to the surface of the wall affect its production in the least, though they may modify its condition and prevent dryness and brittleness.

The sole grows in much the same way as the wall, but it wears quite differently. It never becomes overgrown to the extent seen in some instances of the wall. The hard firm structure of the wall, if not worn down by friction on roads or dry hard surfaces, may grow to a great length. As a rule, when much overgrown, it splits in the direction of its fibres and becomes detached in broken fragments. The sole, when overgrown, has a tendency to become detached in flakes, and never very much exceeds its normal thickness without becoming dry and brittle, when the movements of the horse cause it to break up and fall off.

The frog when it takes a bearing on the ground wears off in shreds. A frog which takes no bearing dries up, and sometimes a large superficial layer is cast off. Though the softest of the horny divisions of the hoof, the frog is able to withstand wear and tear as well as any of the others. Being elastic and resting upon soft tissues, it is able to yield to any undue pressure and leave the firmer horn of the wall and bars to sustain the greater strain. The growth of the frog depends a great deal upon the form of the back parts of the wall. If the heels become overgrown, the frog is removed from bearing and consequently wastes. High heels have always between them a small frog. On the other hand low weak heels have always a large frog, and the explanation is that the increased bearing thrown on the frog causes greater development.

Properties of Horn. Horn is light, hard, tough, and elastic, properties most essential to its usefulness as a protector of the foot. Horn is porous, and absorbs moisture. Too much moisture in horn weakens it, and therefore it must be remembered that the natural protection against this is the hard outer layer of the hoof.   When this layer is rasped off moisture is more easily absorbed until the dry, hard surface is restored by exposure and friction.

Horn is a bad conductor of heat, and thus an equally good protective against the effects of snow in some countries, and of hot dry sands in others.   With a sound thick hoof the application of a red-hot shoe produces very little effect on the internal structures, provided, of course, it remain in contact only a reasonable time.   With a foot protected by a thin layer of horn, fitting a red-hot shoe must be done quickly or it may damage the soft tissues.

DISSECTION OF THE FOOT.

So far we have only described the outer covering of the foot and the structure from which it grows and by which it is connected to the parts within.   A little deeper examination is necessary to understand the mechanism of the whole organ.

If we divide into two lateral halves a foot cut off at the fetlock joint, we have a section which should show the whole of the deeper structures.   In the centre we see the three lower bones of the limb—the pastern, coronet, and pedal.   (Fig. 11).   On the front surface of these bones we

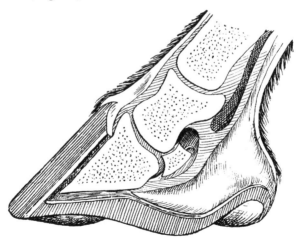

Fig. 11.—Section of Foot.

notice a tendon or sinew which comes from above the knee and is fixed to the upper part of the pedal bone.   At the back of the bones two very large tendons run down and are fixed on the last two bones. These tendons are the structures through which the movements of the foot are made. They have in themselves no power of contraction but they are connected above the knee, and in the hind leg above the hock, to powerful muscles which possess the power of con-contraction. When these muscles contract the tendons are drawn up towards knee or hock, and so move the foot backwards or forwards.

To permit movement of one bone upon another the ends of the bones are suitably shaped, and covered with a layer of gristle or cartilage. To limit the movement and to hold the bones together the ends of each bone are surrounded by ligaments, and thus we have joints formed.

The pastern bone is altogether above the level of the foot, the coronet bone is partially within the hoof, and the joint between it and the pedal bone is quite within. The pedal, often called the coffin bone, (Fig. 12) is entirely within the

Fig. 12.—Side view of **Pedal Bone.**

hoof and fills the front part of the horny envelope completely. It is a peculiarly shaped bone, being continued backwards by two projections which follow the course of the wall to a little beyond the quarters of the foot. (Fig. 13). From this point to the extremity of the heels the wall is not supported by bone but by strong plates of gristle, which are called the lateral cartilages.

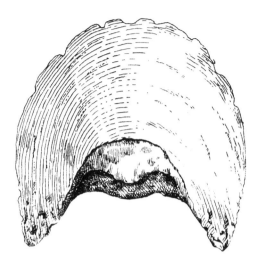

Fig. 13.—Under surface of Pedal Bone.

The Lateral Cartilages are situated one on either side of the foot partly within and partly without the hoof. They form the basis upon which the back part of the wall is moulded, and being elastic permit a certain amount of movement in the posterior parts of the foot. (Fig. 14.)

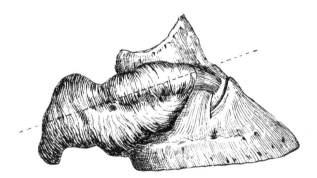

Fig. 14.—The Lateral Cartilage.

If the coffin bone filled the whole hoof, the foot would be too rigid. With bone at the front portion we have a firm surface for attachment, and with cartilage at the back we have an equally firm attachment, but one that will yield to blows or pressure and thus better protect the internal parts. These cartilages extend above the level of the hoof, and may be easily felt in the living horse at the back part of the coronet. (Fig. 15) Between them, and behind the body of the coffin bone is a large space which is filled up by a mass of soft tissue to which various names have been given, such as plantar-cushion, frog-pad, etc.

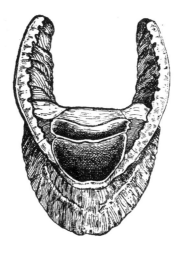

Fig. 15.—Coffin Bone and Lateral Cartilages seen from above.

The Frog-Pad is the name under which we shall notice it. It forms the bulbs of the heels and is the soft basis upon which is spread the sensitive frog It extends from side to side of the foot between the two lateral cartilages, and fills up all the space within the hoof behind the body of the coffin bone. The structure of this pad may be descibed roughly as consisting of a network of fibrous bands, having the interstices filled up with elastic tissue. (Fig. 16.) Down the centre of the pad runs a vertical partition of inelastic fibres ; from this strong fibrous bands pass to each cartilage, and so the whole of the back part of the foot is tied together.   The heels and quarters may be pressed together to some extent, but they are prevented from being forced asunder by the fibrous con- nections of the frog-pad.   During progression the downward movement of the coronet bone is provided for by this soft pad, and so is an upward movement of the frog when excessive bearing is placed upon it

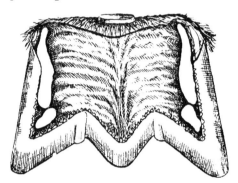

Fig. 16.—Section of foot showing the frog-pad and at each side
the cut edge of the lateral cartilage.

The frog-pad serves other purposes besides those we have just referred to.   It is essentially a cushion or pad to prevent jar or concussion, but it also plays an important part in the action of the foot, as we shall see later on.

The Coronary Cushion or Pad is another mass of tissue of a similar nature to the frog-pad.   It is situated just above the upper border of the hoof, and gives to the coronet its prominence and elasticity.   At this part of the foot there is an enormous number of small blood-vessels and nerves, and the coronary pad forms not only a base for these to rest on but a necessary protection for them.   If instead of this elastic bed they were placed merely between the skin and the hard bones and tendons of the part, they would be injured by every slight bruise.   Even with this cushion, we have in in practice very many serious conditions following bruise of the coronet.

Blood-vessels of the Foot.   It is not necessary to describe the course of these vessels.   All we need remember is that every part of the tissues within the hoof is very plentifully supplied with blood, and that the flow of blood is most rapid when the foot is in action. In a dead foot from which the blood has escaped a certain amount of movement of the bones within the hoof is easily effected. In the living foot when every vessel is filled with blood no such movement takes place. The blood in the vessels forms a sort of water-bed which assists in preventing concussion and which distributes evenly over the whole organ the pressure applied when weight is thrown on the foot In studying the dead foot with a view to understand its mechanism we must not lose sight of the difference which results from having in one case the blood-vessels empty, and in the other—the living animal—the blood-vessels full.

THE FOOT AS A WHOLE.

The details I have given of the structure and uses of each separate part of the foot will, I hope, be sufficient to enable us to understand the form and action of the organ as a whole.

No one part of the foot is of greater importance than another, each is dependent for its highest development and soundest condition upon the integrity of neighbouring parts.

A weak wall allows of the flattening and spreading of the sole, whilst a weak sole permits contraction of the wall. Overgrown heels cause wasting of the frog, but low weak heels are usually accompanied by excessive development of frog.

The special function of the foot is to sustain the weight of the animal whilst standing or moving. The horse standing squarely on all four feet rests his weight chiefly on the lower circumference of the wall. On level ground the sole, on account of its arched form, takes no direct bearing, but if sole and wall be sound a proportion of all pressure applied to the wall is transmitted to the sole. So also must all weight imposed on the arch of the sole be transmitted, through its abutments or union with the wall, to the wall. If the sole be so thin that it yields to pressure then its proper action is destroyed, and instead of acting like an arch and supporting weight imposed on it, it yields and injury results. The arched form of the sole indicates that it was not intended to take a direct bearing on hard ground. On a soft surface the edge of the wall sinks and the whole under surface of the foot takes a direct bearing. Pressure of the sole on the soft surface does no harm because it is diffused evenly over the whole of the sole. We take advantage of this when the wall is diseased or injured, and we desire to throw on the sole a larger share of weight. We turn such animals out into a soft field or stable them on sand or saw-dust. Any system of shoeing founded upon the true form and action of the foot must recognise the arch, and not endeavour to force the sole to take a bearing for which it is not adapted. There is only one part of the sole which should act as a bearing surface, viz., that outer border which is firmly joined to the wall. This part—the abutment of the arch—is destined by nature to take a bearing and through the whole of the sole supports its share of weight

The frog takes a bearing on the ground but it has a weight sustaining function quite secondary to the harder and firmer parts of the hoof. It is formed of a softer horn, and it has above it only soft tissues which permit yielding. The frog then, when weight is placed upon it by the standing horse, recedes from pressure and leaves the heels (wall and bars) to sustain the primary weight Wall, sole, and frog, each take their share in supporting weight, but this function is distributed over them in different degrees, and it is fulfilled by each in a varying manner. During progression the foot is repeatedly raised from and replaced on the ground. It has not only to support weight but to sustain the effects of contact with the ground at each step, and the effects of being the point of resistance when the body is carried forward and the foot is again raised from the ground.

What part of the foot comes first to the ground? Many different answers have been given to this question. It has been said by some that the toe first touches the ground, by others that the foot is laid flat down, and by a few that the heel is the first part to come in contact with the ground. Fortunately it is not now necessary to argue this question on a purely theoretical basis. Instantaneous photography has shown that on level ground, at all paces, the horse touches the ground first with the heel. This fact gives significance to the structual differences we find between the front and back portions of the foot. At the back part of the foot we have the wall thinner than elsewhere, we have the moveable and elastic frog, the lateral cartilages, and the frog-pad. We have in fact a whole series of soft and elastic structures so arranged as to provide a mechanism best adapted to meet shock and to avoid concussion. Whilst drawing heavy loads, or ascending or descending hills, the horse may vary his action to suit the circumstances, and then we have the exception which proves the rule—then we have sometimes the heel, sometimes the toe brought first to the ground.

At the time when the foot first touches the ground, the leg is extended forward and the pastern is in the same oblique position to the shank as when a horse is standing. This obliquity of the pastern is another safeguard against concussion, and it renders impossible the first contact with the ground at any point other than at the heel. As the leg becomes straightened, the weight of the body is imposed upon the foot, but the greatest strain arrives just before the toe leaves the ground, for then there is not only weight to sustain, but the friction to be borne which results from the toe being the fulcrum upon which falls the whole effect of the muscular effort necessary to raise and carry forward the body of the animal. The front part of the foot is structurally well adapted for its use. It presents the thickest and strongest part of the horny covering, and, as an inside basis, it has the unyielding coffin bone. Thus we have at the toe strength and rigidity—at the heels strength and elasticity.

Another important point in the action of the foot is implied by the question—does it expand when weight is thrown on it? The principles of horse-shoeing require that this question should be answered. There are those who say that the foot does not alternately expand and retract as weight is placed upon or removed from it. There are others who assert that the expansion of the foot is an important natural function that must be provided for in any system of shoeing. It is agreed by most observers that at the upper border of the hoof, more particularly at the heels, expansion does occur. It is when we come to the lower border of the foot that the statements are most conflicting Ordinary measurements taken at this part with calipers or by tracings on paper of the foot when raised from the ground and when resting upon it, show no variations in the width of the foot. These methods of measurement are not sufficiently delicate to be trustworthy. Experimentalists in Germany and in this country have recently used an apparatus by which the slightest variations are detected by electrical contact, and the results are very interesting. These experiments show that in a well-formed, healthy foot the hoof throughout its posterior two-thirds does expand to pressure, and perhaps that the arch of the sole is slightly flattened. This expansion is, however, com-

paratively slight—about equal to the thickness of a sheet
of writing paper—and may practically be disregarded in
considering the best methods of shoeing sound feet.

One result of these experiments is to show what an important part the frog plays in the foot, and also how the
action of one part depends upon the conditions of others.
When the frog rests firmly on the ground and weight is
placed upon the foot expansion occurs, especially at the upper
or coronary border of the hoof. When the frog does not
touch the ground and weight is imposed upon the foot, contraction occurs. The explanation of this difference seems to
be as follows. When weight is placed upon a foot, the
coronet bone is depressed upon the soft mass of the frog-pad.
With a sound frog taking a bearing upon the ground, the
frog-pad cannot descend, and the compression to which it is
therefore submitted causes it to bulge laterally and so expand
the back of the foot. When the frog does not reach the
ground and weight is placed upon the frog-pad, there is
nothing to prevent it yielding downwards, and in so doing
the fibrous bands connecting together the two lateral cartilages of the foot are depressed and the cartilages drawn
together—hence the contraction of the foot. No better
illustration could be given of the unity of all parts of the
foot, and how one or many parts may suffer if the structure
or function of one be defective.

There is one more movement of the hoof which is possible
and which must be referred to, as it has been made the basis
of a grave error in shoeing. I have said the back part
of the foot is elastic and yielding. If you examine a shoe,
so applied to a foot that an inch or more of its extremity has
no contact with the hoof, you will find that when weight is
rested on that foot the horn yields downwards and comes in
contact with the shoe This simply demonstrates that when
there is nothing to support it the horn at the heels may
be forced downwards It is not a normal action, and in an
unshod foot cannot occur on a level surface. The effect of
this downward movement of the heels is to put a strain on
the horn of the quarters. A shoe so fitted as to permit this
evil is in common use, and no fault is more serious than
thus forcing an unnatural action upon the hoof at every step.
With unintentional irony this piece of bad work has been
called " easing the heels."

In concluding this chapter, I would just repeat that the
natural bearing surface of the horse's foot is the lower edge

of the wall and that portion of the sole immediately in union with it ; that the arch of the sole should not be in contact with the ground ; that the frog ought to have a bearing on the ground, but ought not to be so prominent as to unduly share in sustaining weight. This natural bearing surface is what we want to utilize in shoeing. We put on a shoe *merely to prevent excessive wear of the hoof.* If we can protect the wall the frog can take care of itself, and we have only so to apply our shoe that we do not damage any useful structure or interfere with any natural function.

NOTE.—No person is expected to learn the structure of a foot entirely from this description. He must obtain two feet cut off at the fetlock joint. One he should soak in water till the hoof can be pulled off. The sensitive foot is then visible and the inside of the hoof ; with these before him, the drawings and descriptions in this chapter will be of great assistance. The second foot he should have sawn vertically down the middle through the point of the toe, and again across the quarters, so as to show the inside of the foot from two different points of view ; this will afford a view of the relation of parts.

CHAPTER III.

PREPARATION OF THE FOOT.

The cheap wisdom of the amateur is often expressed in the remark " the shoe should be fitted to the foot, not the foot to the shoe." Like many other dogmatic statements this is only the unqualified assertion of half a truth. Foot and shoe have to be fitted to each other. There are very few horses whose feet do not require considerable alteration before a shoe can be properly fitted to them. As a rule, when a horse arrives at the forge, the feet are overgrown and quite out of proportion. In a few cases—as when a shoe has been lost on a journey—the foot is worn or broken and irregularly deficient in horn. In either instance the farrier has to make altera- tions in the hoof to obtain the best bearing surface before he fits a new shoe. The claim often made for some novel in- ventions in horse shoes, " that they may be fitted and applied in the stable by a groom or stableman " is evidence of a sad misunderstanding of the art of horse-shoeing. If shod feet always remained of the same shape replacement of shoes would be a very easy matter—but they never do. The living foot is constantly changing, and therefore the man entrusted with fitting shoes to it, must know what its proper form should be. When he finds it disproportionately over- grown he must know how much horn to remove—where to take away and where to leave alone. He must not carry in his head a theoretical standard of a perfect foot and attempt to reduce all feet to that shape. He must make allowance for varieties of feet, and for many little differences of form that present themselves in practice. He has, in fact, to prepare the foot for a shoe, and it is just as important to do this properly as it is to prepare a shoe for the foot. To fit a shoe to a foot which has not been properly prepared may be even more injurious to the horse than " to fit the foot to the shoe."

The general principle to be followed is—to remove super- fluous horn, to obtain a good bearing surface for a shoe, to bring all parts of the hoof equally into proportion. A good foot so prepared, when the horse is standing on level ground should show, when looked at from the front, both sides of the wall of equal height ; the transverse line of the coronet should be parellel with the line of the lower border of the hoof, and the perpendicular line of the leg should cut those lines at right angles. (Fig. 17.) When looked at from the side the

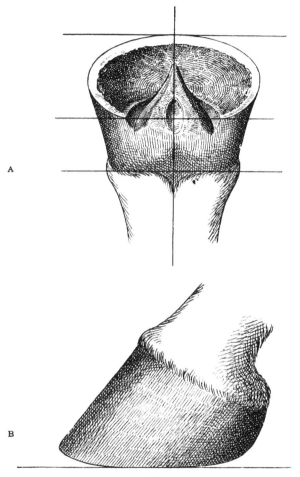

Fig. 17.

height of the heels and the toe should be proportionate. When looked at from behind the frog should be seen touching the ground. On lifting the foot a level bearing surface wider than the wall should be presented, extending from heel to toe all round the circumference of the hoof; within this level border, the sole should be concave, strong, and rough.

In Fig. 17 is shown the foot on its ground surface and from the side. The parallel lines are quite arbitrary, but assist in explaining how the proportion of the foot is to be attained. Both sides of the foot are of the same height. The bearing surface just meets the middle line. All the lines at coronet, heel, and toe, are at right angles to the perpendicular line. The side view shows the proportionate height of heel and toe, and the slope of the wall in front. Compared with Figs. 22 and 23 deviations from proportion are seen.

These conditions are not attainable with all feet, but the prudent farrier does the best he can under the circumstances. It is easy to make the frog touch the ground by over-lowering the heels, but this is only introducing one evil in attempting to avoid another. Some feet have naturally a long toe with an excessive slope of the front part of the wall. To hide this defect a farrier may "stump up" the toe and leave the heels too high, but he does so at the expense of the horse's foot. Each foot requires treating with full knowledge of the form best adapted to its natural formation, and most capable of carrying a shoe.

The Instruments used to prepare a foot for shoeing are a rasp, a drawing knife, and a toeing knife.

The rasp is the most indispensable. It should be sixteen inches long, proportionately broad, and one part of it should be a file-surface. The shorter, narrow rasps do not afford all the advantages a farrier should possess to enable him to do the best work. To strike an even all-round level bearing surface on a hoof a farrier requires a large rasp, just as a joiner must have a large plane to produce a level surface on wood. Harm may be done by the careless use of a rasp, and a bearing-surface spoiled by the over-reduction of horn at one place. This fault may be aggravated by attempts to mend it, if such attempt take the form of further reduction of the whole hoof on a foot where horn is deficient.

The drawing knife is a comparatively modern instrument which replaced a tool called the buttress. A drawing knife is formed with great skill for the purpose of paring out the concave sole of the hoof, and has done infinite harm. In the days which have now almost passed away, when it was thought the proper thing to make the hoof look clean, smooth, and pretty, the drawing knife was the chief instrument in the preparation of the foot. Now, when nearly all men know that the stronger the sole and frog of the foot can be preserved the better for the horse, this knife is less used—and the less the better. The doorman, preparing a foot for the fireman to fit a shoe to, should not use a knife at all. The man who fits the shoe requires a knife to remove occasional little prominences of horn which are liable to cause uneven pressures or which are in the way of a properly fitted shoe—as, for instance, the edge of the wall to make way for a clip, or the angle of sole at the heel to prevent uneven pressure by the shoe.

The toeing knife usually consists of about a foot of an old sword-blade. This knife is held and guided by one hand of the farrier, whilst with the other it is driven through overgrown horn by the hammer. Skilfully used it is un-objectionable, and for the large strong hoof of heavy draught horses it saves a great deal of time and labour. For the lighter class of horses it is unnecessary, and for weak feet with a thin horn covering it is dangerous.

The toeing knife cannot leave a finished level bearing surface, and its work has to be completed by a few strokes of the rasp. A farrier should, therefore, never attempt to remove all the superfluous horn with the knife, he should leave some for the rasp so that in producing the final level surface no encroachment upon the necessary thickness of covering horn need be made.

The overgrown foot such as we find on a healthy horse that has retained a set of shoes for some weeks, or that has been without shoes on a surface not hard enough to cause sufficient wear, is quite unfitted to receive a shoe. It must be reduced to proportions. In Fig. 18, I have

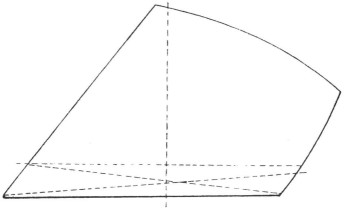

Fig. 18.

attempted to show diagrammatically a side view of an overgrown hoof. The dotted lines at the base show two effects of
lowering one part more than another, although both attain a
level surface. In Fig. 21 we see the result of over-lowering the
heels, and in Fig. 20 of leaving them too high. It may also be
noticed that these conditions affect other parts of the foot; in fact
not only other parts but the whole foot, and even the relative
position of the foot to the leg. If we compare the proportionate foot, Fig. 19, with the diagram Fig. 21. it will
be seen that by over-lowering the heels the slope of the front
of the foot is increased, that the bearing surface from heel
to toe is slightly increased in length, and that if the dotted
perpendicular line be accepted as showing the direction
through which the weight of the body passes, lowering the
heels tends to put an increased proportion of weight on the
back parts of the foot. If we compare Fig. 19 with Fig. 20
we see the effect of leaving the heels too high. The bearing
surface from heel to toe is shortened, the slope of the wall
at the toe is made less, and more weight is thrown upon the
front parts of the foot.

Now these alterations in both cases affect not only the
form of the foot but its relative position to the leg, and
as the bones of the limb above are a series of levers connected
by muscles and ligaments so placed as to be most efficient
for movement, it is evident that alterations of the foot must
affect the action of the limb. (Compare Figs. 19, 20 and 21) In
the unshod horse roaming about there is a natural automatic
return to proper relative position whenever it has been
temporarily upset. A long toe is worn down and high heels
are reduced to their proper level by friction. Not so a
foot protected by an iron shoe. Wear is stopped, and a
disproportionate hoof becomes more and more disproportionate. Temporary alterations of the position of the
foot do little harm because they are permitted, within a
margin, by the movement of joints and by the elasticity of
muscles. When, however, an alteration of position is
continued for many weeks it tends to become permanently
fixed and may thus do a great deal of harm, which is not
traced to its real cause because the effect is slow and gradual.
It is important, therefore, to remember that the proportion
of the hoof is to be maintained not only because it is
necessary to the well-being of the foot; but because it affects
the action of the whole limb. Too long a toe may cause
a horse to stumble, and it must always increase the strain

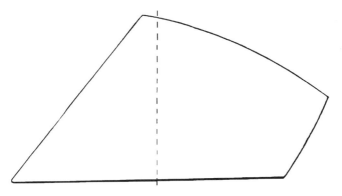

Fig. 19.—A proportionate hoof.

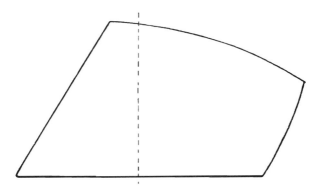

Fig. 20.—A disproportionate hoof—heels too high.

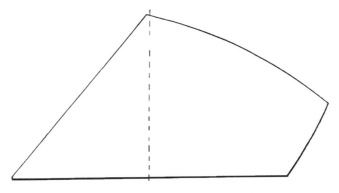

Fig. 21.—A disproportionate hoof—heels too low.

on the back tendons during progression. Heels too high prevent the frog from taking its proper bearing on the ground, and thus cause a loss of function in the back parts of the foot. An excessively high heel has a tendency to throw the knee forward and to straighten the pastern.

It is impossible to lay down any hard and fast rule to guide a farrier in maintaining the proportions of heel and toe when reducing an overgrown hoof to proper form. Feet differ much in their natural formation, some are high-heeled and some low, some are straight in front some very much

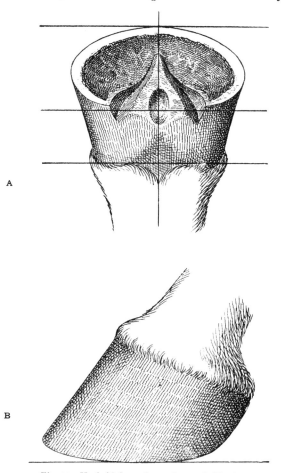

Fig. 22.—Heels high—under surface and side view.

sloped, some are narrow and upright, others round and spreading. In Fig. 22 the heels are too high, and the bearing surface does not reach the transverse line at the heels. The side view shows the excessive height of heels and the slope of the wall in front too upright. Great assistance is afforded the farrier in judging whether he should remove more horn from heel or toe by the appearance of the under surface of the foot. When the heels are much above the level of the frog there is an indication

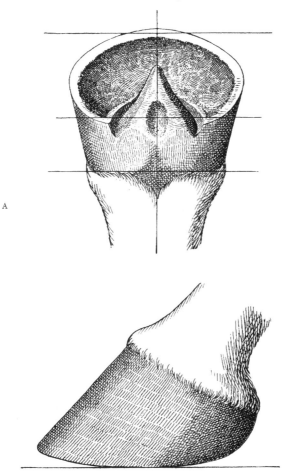

A

Fig. 23.—Heels low—toe long.

for their lowering. When the wall and bars are about flush with the angle of sole between them, there is, as a rule, no more horn to spare at that part. The length of the toe may be usefully gauged by the condition of the junction between wall and sole   When the sole is sound and strong all the wall above its level—wall unsupported by sole and showing on its inner aspect marks of the horny laminæ—may be rasped down so that a firm bearing surface is obtained consisting of wall and sole.

In Fig. 23 the bearing surface at the heels is below the line marking a proportionate foot. The toe is too long and projects beyond the transverse toe line. The side view shows the low heel and the corresponding excess in the slope of the wall in front. The lower transverse line in each figure does not represent the ground, but is added to make clear the height of heels and length of toe.

Important as it is to maintain the relative proportions between the front and back parts of the foot, it is perhaps even more important to preserve the balance between the two sides of a foot. Both sides must be left of equal height. If one side be higher than the other a disproportionate amount of weight is thrown on the lower side, and more or less strain is put upon the ligaments of the joint above. In the Figs. 24 one limb is shown with both sides of the

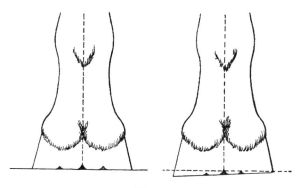

Fig. 24

hoof even, and the straight line of the limb cuts squarely across the transverse line of the bearing surface of the foot. In the the other limb one side of the hoof is too high, and in the preparation for shoeing only that side will require attention.

Through constant neglect of this point some feet become more or less permanently twisted—and the twist occurs at the coronet. The ground surface of a foot or a shoe always tends to remain at right angles to the direction of the limb, and when the sides of a hoof are allowed to remain of unequal height, the higher side presses the soft tissues of the coronet upwards. As the hoof grows from the coronet the side thus increased in height is not so noticeably uneven at the lower border of the wall as at its upper, and it cannot be restored to its proper form, except by months of careful attention and slight over-lowering at each shoeing. The diagrams (Figs. 25 and 26) represent vertical sections through a foot from side to side. One shows the wall uneven at the base, the other shows it uneven at the coronet.

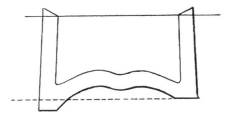

Fig. 25.—Uneven at ground surface.

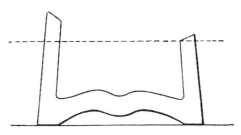

Fig. 26.—Uneven at coronet.

Peculiarities in the formation of a limb sometimes cause an apparent error in the relative position of the foot. Thus we have horses that turn their toes in, and those that turn their toes out. The cause of this twist takes place at the upper part of the limb, and it will be found that when the toes turn out the elbow turns in and *vice versâ*. The farrier can do no good to this formation, and attempts to alter it or disguise it by devices in shoeing are only injurious to the foot,—little deceptions worthy of a horse-coper.

A good bearing surface is the primary object aimed at in preparing the foot for a shoe. The relative position of the limb to the foot and the proper proportions of every part of the foot are matters to be borne in mind whilst the farrier is directly forming the bearing surface for a shoe. A good bearing surface must be even, level, on sound horn, and as wide as can be obtained to give stability to the shoe. It should not be limited to the wall. If, without over-reduction, the use of the rasp leaves a firm portion of the sole as a level surface continuous with the lower edge of the wall, the best of bearing surfaces is obtained. (Fig. 27.) The bearing

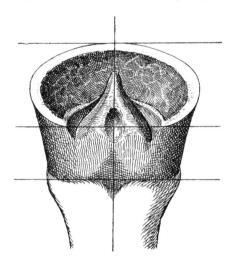

Fig. 27.

surface should be level from heel to toe, and no part of it can be singled out either as unfit to bear weight or as specially capable of enduring undue pressure. No broken or diseased horn should be used as bearing surface for a shoe. The broken horn should be removed and the diseased horn must, it not entirely removed, have so much of its border cut or rasped off as will prevent contact with a shoe.

After forming a level bearing surface with the rasp the sharp outer border of the wall is lightly removed with the file, so as to prevent splitting of the horn. The outer surface of the wall should not be rasped for it affords protection to the deeper layer of horn. The harder the outer layer of horn is kept the tougher and firmer is the whole thickness.

The Sole and Frog require very little attention. No sensible farrier now puts himself to the unnecessary trouble of cutting away horn that is wanted for protection. It was not the practical farrier that introduced the stupid "paring and cutting" that ruined horses' feet for nearly a century. It was the theorists, who taught expansion of the wall and descent of the sole as primary necessities in the function of a foot, who must be credited with all the evils resulting from robbing the sole and frog of horn. When a horse is shod with an iron shoe the wall cannot wear, and therefore it has to be artificially reduced at each shoeing. But the shoe does not interfere with the wear of a frog, and the farrier may safely leave that organ entirely to take care of itself. To some extent the shoe does interfere with the natural wear of the sole, and, therefore, any flakes of horn which have been prevented by the shoe from detaching themselves from the sole may be removed. The best way to remove these is with the buffer. The sole should not be pared out. I mean not only that the horn should be left strong, it should not be pared with a drawing knife, even if only a harmless surface layer be removed. The effect of leaving the sole of a shod foot with a smooth, level, pared surface is to stop its natural method of throwing off more or less broken flakes, and to cause it to retain that which is half loose until it is removed in one great cake

A portion of the sole that requires a little special care in preparing for shoeing is the angle between the wall and the bars — the well-known seat of "corn." This must not be left so as to come in contact with the shoe. It is not to be "scooped" out, but it should be reduced distinctly below the level of the wall so that when the shoe has been in position for a week or two there is still no contact between the horn of the soles and the iron at that point.

Level or adjusted surface? The bearing surface of a hoof must, of course, be exactly adapted to the surface of shoe intended to be applied. Presuming that the best surface for a shoe is one level from toe to heel, I have insisted upon the necessity of a level bearing surface on the foot. There are, however, exceptional cases in which a level shoe is not used, and then we must alter the foot accordingly. Horses that wear the toe of a shoe out of all proportion to the rest of the iron may be beneficially shod with a shoe turned up at the toe. To fit such a shoe the hoof surface must not be made level, it must be rasped away at the toe and rounded off to follow the line of the shoe. In the three diagrams (Fig. 28.) is shown—(*a*) side view of a foot prepared to suit the turned-up shoe at the toe, (*b*) a level line to fit a level shoe and, (*c*) a form often adopted on the Continent to suit a shoe fitted with a slight

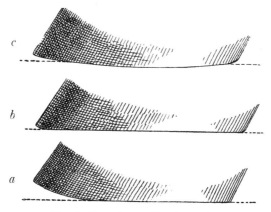

Fig. 28.—Three forms of bearing-surface.

curve throughout. This adjusted shoe is designed to imitate the shape of the worn surface of an old shoe or to some extent the worn surface of an unshod foot. Every farrier knows how many horses go better after a level shoe has been worn a few days than when first applied, and it is argued, with reason, that the greater ease is due to the shoe being worn to the form offering least resistance to the movement of the foot in locomotion. I have nothing to say against this form of shoe and the necessary form of foot surface for it, except that it is more difficult to make than the ordinary level one. When adopted the curve of the foot should not be obtained by over-lowering the toe and heels but by leaving the quarters higher.

FAULTS TO BE AVOIDED.

Fig. 29 shows a hoof in which shortening of the toe has been effected not by reducing the ground surface of the wall, but by rasping away the wall in front of the toe. This should not be done with any good foot, but it may be adopted with feet having an unnaturally long toe and no superfluous horn on the under surface. A " stumped-up " toe is very ugly and it weakens the hoof in front.

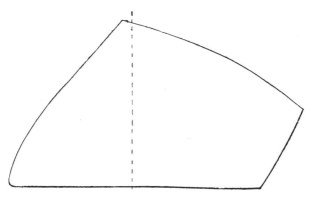

Fig. 29.—A " stumped-up " toe.

Uneven bearing surfaces are easily produced by a careless use of the rasp. One side of the wall may be made lower than the other, one heel may be reduced more than the rest of the foot, or one side of the toe may be unevenly reduced. In Fig. 30 the foot presents an uneven surface

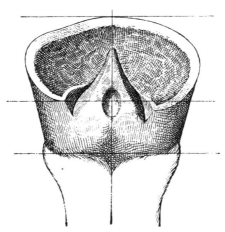

Fig. 30.—Uneven surface.

which not uncommonly results from careless work. The parts over-reduced are those most easily reached with a rasp. The near foot suffers at the outside heel and inside toe. The off foot at the inside heel and outside toe. A left handed farrier would injure the feet in just the opposite positions.

Another fault results from holding the rasp untruly.   If we suppose the inside heel of the near foot to be under preparation and the farrier inclines his rasp too much inwards, he leaves the wall at the heel lower than the sole within it. On such a foot a level shoe rests upon the sole instead of upon the wall, and a bruised heel soon follows.

Paring away the sole to produce a deep concave appearance has another evil effect in addition to that before pointed out.   It removes the horn just within the border of the wall, taking away the natural support, and leaving as bearing surface for a shoe a narrow ridge instead of a strong flat surface   Fig. 31 shows this fault, and it must be remembered that this ridge may be left as thin as a knife edge. Such a ridge cannot sustain the weight of the horse, and when it yields the shoe also yields, the clenches are raised and the shoe becomes loose.

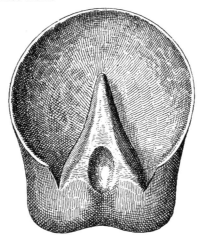

Fig. 31.—A Pared-out Sole.

Excessive rasping of Wall.   The best farriers—those most proud of their work—have a great temptation to use a rasp too freely to the outer surface of the wall.   The hoof gets rough, or it may be ridged, its appearance is improved by being made smooth, and it is only human to turn out work which is clean and neat.   Owners and grooms are rather inclined to forget the claims of the horse when judging shoeing, and the result is that some harm is done by excessive rasping.   A strong foot does not suffer much, but its strength is preserved by leaving the hard outer surface intact. Rasping off an outer layer of horn favours evaporation and hardening of the underneath layer, and the toughness so desirable is to some degree replaced by hardness and brittleness. Excessive rasping below the clenches is even more injurious than rasping above them. The wall, between its bearing surface and the clenches, has to withstand the contact of the shoe, and the perforation by nails It should be the toughest and strongest part, and, therefore, should not be rasped more than is necessary to lay down the clenches and finish the fitting. Unfortunately the neatest work is done by fitting a shoe " close " and then rasping off any protruding horn. This is bad for the foot, as it weakens the wall and spoils the bearing surface at each shoeing. The worst offenders in this direction are dealers, who sacrifice everything to appearances and insist upon shoeing being neat at all hazards.

Opening the Heels is one of the gravest faults a farrier can be guilty of. It consists in cutting away the extremity of the wall at the heel and generally a slice off the side of the frog at the same time. The effect is to produce an appearance of width at the back of the foot—to make what is called " a fine open foot." Fig. 31 shows a foot which has been injured in this way. The wedge shaped opening which results has many objections. It breaks the continuity of structures at the heels, it removes horn unnecessarily, it weakens the foot and, when the wall is interfered with, it shortens the bearing surface for a shoe. The bearing surface at the back of the foot is perhaps the most important of any afforded by the wall. The longer the bearing surface is at the heels the more the base for sustaining weight is brought under the leg, and the better the position for supporting the body. All removal of horn that shortens this surface is injurious.

Over-reduction of hoof is always a fault. It is true a carefully fitted shoe on a foot so treated may do no harm for a time. Too much horn should be left rather than too little. A strong covering of horn is a protection against many mistakes in the fitting or form of a shoe applied to a foot. So long as a hoof is everywhere strong enough to sustain pressure and afford bearing, weight is evenly distributed throughout the whole foot. When the horn is thin it yields to any uneven pressure and damage is done to the foot, even if immediate lameness is not induced.

CHAPTER IV.

THE FORM AND MANUFACTURE OF SHOES.

Horse-shoes are made either by hand or machinery. In this country most are hand-made—the front shoes from new bar-iron, and the hind from old shoes welded together and drawn out under heavy hammers Probably no method of working iron gives such good results as this in producing a hard, tough shoe that will withstand wear. The custom of the trade is to keep a stock of shoes suitable for all the regular customers. From this stock are selected sizes and forms, which are then specially fitted for each foot.

Various materials have been tried in the production of horse-shoes. Leather, compressed and hardened, has been tried, and failed. Vulcanite was experimented with unsuccessfully. Paper, or more correctly, a compressed *papier maché*, has also been tested but proved unsatisfactory. Steel has been pretty largely tried in many different forms, but it is difficult to temper. As nearly all shoes are applied immediately after being fitted they have to be rapidly cooled in water, and steel treated in this way is made so hard that, if the shoes do not break, they are dangerously slippery on most paved streets. As a material for shoes good malleable iron has no equal. It can be obtained in bars of various sizes to suit any form and weight of shoe, and the old shoes made from it may be worked up over and over again.

The chief objects to be attained in any particular pattern or form of shoe are—that it be light, easily and safely retained by few nails, capable of wearing three weeks or a month, and that it afford good foot-hold to the horse. All shoes should be soundly worked and free from flaws.

The first shoes were doubtless applied solely to protect the foot from wear. The simplest arrangement would then be either a thin plate of iron covering the ground surface of the foot, or a narrow rim fixed merely round the lower border of the wall. Experience teaches that these primitive forms can be modified with advantage, and that certain patterns are specially adapted to our artificial conditions. A good workman requires no directions as to how he should work, and it is doubtful if a bad one would be benefitted by any

written rules, but it should be noted that a well-made shoe
may be bad for a horse's foot, whilst a very rough, badly-made
one may, when properly fitted, be a useful article.   To make
and apply horse-shoes a man must be more than a clever
worker in iron—he must be a farrier, and that necessitates a
knowledge of the horse's foot and the form of shoe best
adapted to its wants.

Weight of Shoes.   The lighter a shoe can be made
the better.   Weight is a disadvantage we are obliged to put
up with to obtain wear, for the frequent removal of shoes is
only a little less injurious to the hoof than working with none
at all.   It is not to be understood that the heaviest shoe gives
the most wear ; on the contrary, a heavy shoe may have the
iron so distributed as to increase the rapidity of wear, and
a shoe of half the weight properly formed may last longer.
It is no uncommon thing to find worn-out shoes still weighing
more than a new shoe which will, on the same horse, give a
longer period of wear.   When a horse wears his shoes out
very rapidly, the indication to the farrier is not simply to
increase the weight, but to see if he can obtain more wear by
altering the form and distributing the iron in a different way.
A tired horse wears his shoes much more rapidly than a fresh
and active one.   Continued slipping wears away a shoe out of
all proportion to the work done by a horse having a firm foot-
hold.   These two different conditions may be partially due to
the shoes, for a heavy shoe tires the leg, and broad flat shoes
favour slipping.   Some horses wear one special part of the
shoe excessively—as a rule, either at the toe or the heel—and
this is better met by turning up the worn part out of the
line of wear than by thickening it and so increasing weight.
Besides, a heavy shoe requires a greater number or a larger
size of nails to retain it securely in position, and this is a
disadvantage.   It has often been asserted that a horse " goes
better " in a heavy shoe than a light one, and that this is due
to the heavier shoe acting as a protection to the foot and
warding off concussion.   If the term " goes better " merely
means that he lifts his foot higher and consequently bends his
knee more, I do not deny the assertion.   The reason of this
is not that the horse feels less concussion and therefore goes
freer.   It is an exaggeration of the natural movements, due
simply to the horse with weight imposed on his feet having
to use the muscles of his arms more to lift that weight.   The
same thing can be brought about by tying bags of shot on to
the hoof, which is done to cultivate " action."   The healthy

foot requires no artificial aids against concussion, but when a foot becomes tender from bad shoeing it may sometimes be relieved by adding to the substance and weight of a shoe.

The following are about the average weights, per shoe, of horses standing 16 hands high:

Race Horses ...	2 to 4	ounces.
Hacks and Hunters	15 to 18	,,
Carriage Horses ...	20 to 30	,,
Omnibus ,, ...	3 to $3\frac{1}{2}$	lbs.
Dray ,, ...	4 to 5	,,

Thickness and Width of Shoes. To obtain the necessary amount of wear from shoes they must be increased either in thickness or width, and it will assist us in estimating the relative value of these conditions if we shortly consider their advantages and disadvantages. I may say at once that no sound foot requires a wide shoe merely as "cover" or protection for the sole. Defective soles may sometimes require protection, but sound ones never, and we may therefore put aside entirely all claims made for width of shoe under pretence that it gives a valuable protection to the foot. A shoe should be as wide as the natural bearing surface of the foot, so that it may occupy the whole of the space offered by nature as useful for bearing. Even when it is wider no harm is done until the width is such as to afford a lodgement for stones, etc., between the concave sole and the web of the shoe.

A thick shoe raises the foot from the ground and thus removes the frog from bearing—a very decided disadvantage. It also requires the larger sizes of nails to fill up the deep nail holes, and very often renders the direction of the nail holes a matter of some difficulty.

The width of a shoe may beneficially vary. It should be widest at the toe to afford increased surface of iron where wear is greatest. It should be narrowest at the heels so as not to infringe upon the frog, nor yet to protrude greatly beyond the level of the wall. The thickness of a shoe should not vary unless, perhaps, it be reduced in the quarters. Heel and toe should be of the same thickness so as to preserve a level bearing. Excess of thickness at the toe puts a strain on the back tendons, whilst excess at the heels tends to straighten the pastern.

The surfaces of Shoes. There are two surfaces of the shoe which claim attention, one which is applied to the foot, and another which rests on the ground. The form of these surfaces may be varied greatly, but of course the foot-surface presents much less necessity and less opportunity for alterations than the ground-surface The foot-surface of a shoe must be formed in accordance with the requirements of the horse's foot, and no other consideration should be allowed to materially modify it The ground-surface may be altered to suit the tastes and prejudices of the owner as well as the requirements of the horse and the peculiarity of roadways.

The Foot-Surface. It is quite obvious that the surface of the shoe upon which the hoof has to rest should be regular and even ; that it should not consist of hills and holes or grooves and ridges. I should not have mentioned such a very evident matter but that in large towns, the cheaper and poorer classes of shoeing commonly possess this very fault When shoes are made from thin, wide, old iron tyres they are " buckled " on one surface, and to hide this the farrier puts that side to the foot so that it is not noticed until it causes damage. There are three or four forms of foot-surface adopted by farriers, all of which have distinctive features, and some of which have very grave evils. There is the plain flat surface which is given to all narrow shoes, to hunting shoes, and to some heavier and wider shoes. So

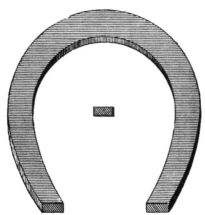

Fig. 32.—A level, flat bearing-surface.

long as the sole is healthy and arched this is a very good form. All hind shoes have a flat foot-surface, and most fore shoes might have it with advantage It utilises the whole of the natural bearing surface, and must of necessity afford a firmer basis for the foot to rest upon than a more limited surface. The fore feet are not so constantly arched in the sole as the hind. Sometimes they are flat and occasionally convex. If a shoe be intended for use on all feet—on feet with convex and flat soles as well as those properly formed— a wide flat foot surface would often cause injury by pressing unevenly upon the sole. To avoid this injury in less than five per cent. of feet, and to save the trouble of keeping in stock shoes of different forms, the flat foot-surface of front shoes has been replaced by a bevelled or " seated " surface. (Fig. 33.)

This form is very widely used. It consists of a narrow flat surface next the outer circumference of the shoe, about equal

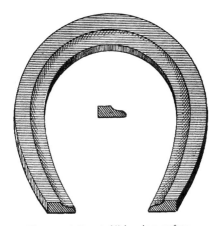

Fig. 33.—A " seated " bearing surface.

in width to the border of the wall, and within that, of a bevelled surface, sloped off so as to avoid any pressure on a flat sole. This " seated " surface is not positively injurious but it limits the bearing to the wall, and neglects to utilise the additional bearing surface offered by the border of the sole. If shoes were to be made all alike no shoe is so generally useful and safe as one with a foot-surface of this form, but it is evident that when the sole of the foot is concave there is nothing gained by making half the foot-surface of the shoe also concave

There are two other forms of foot-surface on shoes. In one the surface slopes gradually from the outer to the inner edge of the shoe, like the side of a saucer. In the other the incline is reversed and runs from the inner edge downwards to the outer. This last form is not often used, and was invented with the object of spreading or widening the foot to which it was attached. The inventor seemed to think that contraction of a foot was an active condition to be overcome by force, and that expansion might be properly effected by a plan of constantly forcing apart the two sides of the foot. The usual result of wearing such a shoe is lameness, and it achieves no good which cannot be as well reached by simply letting the foot alone.

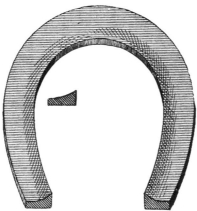

Fig. 34.—Foot-surface sloped outwards.

The foot-surface which inclines downwards and inwards like a saucer acts in an exactly opposite way to the other.

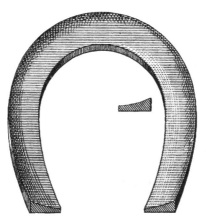

Fig. 35.—Foot-surface sloped inwards.

The wall cannot rest on the outer edge of the shoe, and consequently falls within it, the effect being that at every step the horse's foot is compressed by the saucer-shaped bearing. This form of surface (Fig. 35) is frequently seen, and is at all times bad and unnecessary.   Even when making a shoe for the most convex sole it is possible to leave an outer bearing surface, narrow but level, which will sustain weight without squeezing the foot.

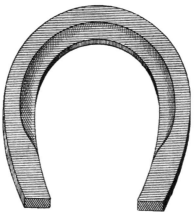

Fig. 36.—Foot-surface level at Heels.

At the heels the foot-surface of all shoes should be flat—not seated—so that a firm bearing may be obtained on the wall and the extremity of the bar.   No foot is convex at the heels, therefore there is no excuse for losing any bearing surface by seating the heels of a shoe to avoid uneven pres- sure.   Fig. 36 rather exaggerates the " unseated " portion of shoe.

The Ground-Surface   As I have said, this may vary indefinitely.   Sometimes it is a plain flat surface, broken only by the holes made for nails or by the " fullering " which affords not only space for the nails but some grip on the ground.   When a shoe is " fullered " the groove made should be deep, so as to let the nail-head well down, and wide so as to afford room for giving the nail a proper direction.   If the fullering be continued round the toe of a shoe by a good workman neatness is given, but when a clip is drawn the iron is so reduced that some wear is sacrificed.   If only an inch at the toe be unfullered, the solid iron affords more wear just where it is wanted.

Fig. 37.—Concave ground-surface.

The concave shoe, often described as a hunting-shoe, presents a very different ground-surface from that just referred to. It rests upon two ridges with the fullering between, and on the inner side of these the iron is suddenly sloped off. This shoe is narrow and flat on the foot-surface, and is specially formed to give a good foothold and to be secure on the hoof.

A Rodway shoe has two longitudinal grooves and three ridges on its ground-surface. The outer groove carries the nails,

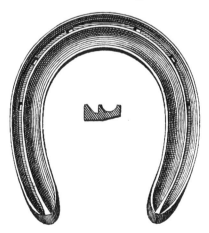

Fig. 38.—Double-grooved ground-surface.

and the inner groove lightens the shoe and increases the foot-hold. It is not the number of grooves or ridges that prevents slipping ; it is the absence of a continuous flat surface of iron, and the existence of irregularities which become filled up with sand and grit   A four-grooved shoe has no more anti-slipping properties than a three-grooved, and a one grooved shoe is as good as either, although it cannot stand the same amount of wear.

Transverse ridges and notches have also been tried as ground-surfaces for shoes, but offer very little, if any, better grip than the longitudinal grooves. Their great disadvantage is that they cannot be made deep enough without weakening the shoe, whilst if shallow they are worn out before the shoe has been long in wear.

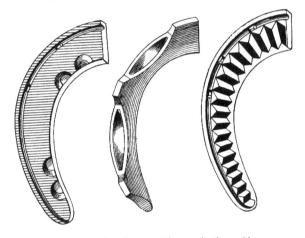

Fig. 38.—Ground-surfaces, notches, projections, ridges.

A Calkin is the name given to the extremity of a shoe when turned down at the heels. Calkins are used on most hind shoes and, in some parts of the country, on fore shoes. They are supposed to be the most convenient and effective means of giving good foot-hold. This supposition is correct when a horse travels on soft ground or on streets so paved that a space is left between each course of stones. They are of very little use on asphalte or wood pavement, and not much more use on roller-made macadam. With light modern carriages and level modern roads calkins are quite unnecessary, and better means of giving foot-hold may be substituted. It is a fact that horses when shoes are new and calkins prominent do their work without slipping, and that when the calkins are worn down the horse moves with less confidence and security. This does not prove that calkins are necessary. It must be remembered that horses possess a power of adapting themselves to circumstances, but having learned to rely upon any artificial assistance they are the more helpless, for a time, on its withdrawal. Calkins assist the horse for a time, but after the calkin is worn down the horse is in a worse position than if he had never become accustomed to its assistance. Of course on soft ground, especially grass, calkins afford a firmer grip than any other contrivance. On the other hand, their constant use lifts the frog out of bearing and causes it to waste, thus spoiling the action of the natural provision against slipping. Level shoes on the hind feet promote sound, prominent frogs, and give firm foothold for all light horses. Even omnibus horses, now that the vehicles are supplied with effective foot-brakes, may advantageously be worked without calkins. On country roads, especially when the district is hilly or the load is heavy, calkins may be requisite, and must then be made to do as little harm as possible.

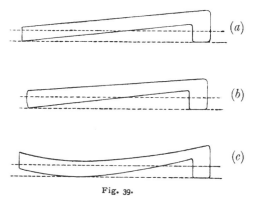

Fig. 39.

The wear of a shoe is affected by the height of a calkin. The more the heel is raised the greater the amount of wear at the toe. Many shoes when worn out at the toe show very little effects of wear at other parts, and the question arises how best to increase the wear of the shoe without increasing its weight. In Fig. 39 three diagrams are presented in which dotted lines show the effect of wear. At (a) the shoe is of even thickness throughout—from heel to toe—and the line of wear shows that when the shoe is worn out a great amount of iron remains. At (*b*) the quarters of the shoe are made thinner and the toe is made thicker, so that with no increase of weight but by a better distribution of the iron, increased wear is provided for at the part where it is most required. At (*c*) is shown a shoe similar in form to that at (*b*) but differently fitted. The toe is turned slightly upwards, and the result is that a larger portion of iron is brought into wear. In the case of very hard-wearing horses that scrape out the toe of the ordinary shoe in ten or fourteen days this form of fitting adds considerably to the durability of the shoe, and so preserves the foot from the evil of too frequent removal of shoes, whilst avoiding any increase of weight Without calkins wear is more evenly distributed, and the toe is not worn away disproportionately to the rest of the shoe.

Fig. 40.—Two calkins—the low square one preferable.

A calkin throws the leg and foot, to some extent, out of their proper position. A very high calkin is not only objectionable, it is unnecessary. Not much prominence is required to afford a catch or stop. Excessive height is usually given to meet wear, and this can be obtained equally well by increasing the width and breadth. I, therefore, recommend that when calkins are used they should be low, square and broad. The further under a foot the calkin is placed, the greater is the raising of the heel, therefore calkins should always be accompanied by a long shoe. The further back a calkin be placed the less it interferes with the natural position of the foot.

Calkins render a horse liable to tread the opposite foot, and the higher and sharper the calkin the greater the injury inflicted. To avoid this injury the inner heel of a shoe frequently has no calkin, but is made at the same level as the outer by narrowing and raising the iron at the heel, forming what is called a wedge heel. This is not an advisable form of shoe as it has on the inner heel a skate-shaped formation, most favourable to slipping, and on the outer a catch—an arrangement tending to twist the foot each time the catch takes hold of the ground. If calkins are used at all they should be of equal height and on both heels of the shoe.

In Scotland, and in the North of England, heavy horses are shod, fore and hind, not only with calkins but also with toe-pieces, and the owners assert that the horses could not do the work without them. That horses do similar work in the South without calkins and toe-pieces rather shakes one's faith in the assertion, but it must be remembered that nearly all paved streets in the North have a division left between the rows of stones in which the toe-piece finds a firm resisting surface. I believe also that the average load drawn is greater in the North than in the South. One thing in favour of toe-pieces must be acknowledged—they, with the calkins, restore the natural position of the foot and preserve the level of the shoe. On the larger draught horses the toe-pieces permit a lighter shoe to be used, as the portion of iron between heels and toe need not be thick to resist wear. It only requires to be strong enough to support weight and much less iron is therefore used.

The heavy dray horse of the North, shod with toe-pieces and calkins, is never worked at a trot. In London all horses are trotted—a proceeding which reflects discredit upon the intelligence of the managers.

I must mention another objection to calkins. They increase the tendency to "cut," and many horses will cease "cutting" after calkins are removed and a level shoe has been adopted.

Nails and nail holes. It is necessary to consider these together as they are dependent on each other. Shoes were first nailed to the feet by flat-headed nails, and probably it was a long time before the wedge-headed nail was thought of. When the nail head fits into the nail hole it may retain the shoe till it is worn as thin as a penny, but if only the shank of the nail enters the shoe, the head is soon worn off and the shoe becomes loose. Within the last 20 years the horse-shoe nail trade has been revolutionised by the introduction of machinery. Machine-made nails are now almost entirely used, and the three or four leading brands are as near perfection as were the very best hand-made. Practically there is no fault to find with them, and as they are ready-pointed for driving they save time and labour in the forge. They are made in various sizes, and numbered from 2 up to 16. Only

the very best iron can be used to produce good nails.
Nothing is dearer than bad nails which cause injury to the
foot and loss of shoes.

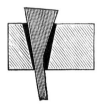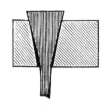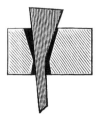

Fig. 41

A good nail should present certain forms of head, neck
and shank. The head should not be too broad at the top or
it may become fixed in the nail-hole only by its upper edge,
as shown in the middle diagram Fig. 41, and when the
shoe has had a few days wear the nail loses its hold,
and the shoe is loose. The neck should not be too thick,
as it is then liable to press on the sensitive foot and to
break the wall. The shank should not be too wide or too
thick. The point should not be too long or too tapered as
this leaves insufficient metal to form a good clinch.

There are two methods of putting nail-holes into shoes —
by "fullering" and by "stamping." A stamped shoe is one
in which the nail holes are merely punched at certain
distances, so as to leave four-sided tapered holes of the exact
shape of a nail-head. A fullered shoe is one having a groove
round the circumference through which the nail-holes are
punched. Both processes, when well-done, admit of nails being
driven into the hoof with equal safety and ease.

Whether stamped or fullered, there are a few more important points to remember about the nail-holes. The wall
is not of the same thickness throughout, but becomes thinner
towards the heels. The inner side of the foot is also some-
what thinner and more upright than the outer. The safest
position, then, for the nails is in the front half of the foot,
but should this position not present sound horn they may
be placed further back. The danger of placing nails near
the heels is due entirely to the greater risk in driving
them through the thin horn. There need be no fear of
interfering with expansion.

The distance of the nail-holes from the outer edge of the
shoe should depend upon the thickness of the horn of the wall,
and therefore be greater in large shoes than in smaller, and
greater at the toe than at the heels of the same shoe. When

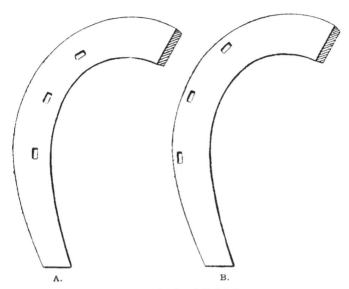

A.   B.

Fig. 42.—Wrongly placed Nail-holes.

the nail-holes are all near to the circumference of the
shoe (Fig. 42 B.) they are described as "fine"; when they
are all placed far from the edge (Fig. 42 A.) they are called
"coarse." When the nail-holes are too "fine" a nail has to
be driven high up in the wall to obtain a firm hold, and
this is liable to split the horn. When nail-holes are too
" coarse " the nail in driving goes dangerously near the sensitive foot. The evils of coarse and fine nailing depend a great
deal upon the method of fitting the shoes. When shoes are
fitted full to the foot (when the outer circumference of the
shoe is greater than the circumference of the wall) " coarse "
nail-holes are brought to about their best position. When
shoes are fitted close (*i.e.*, when their outer edge is brought
within the border of the wall) "fine " nail-holes are brought
to their best position in relation to the foot. It need hardly
be added that the fit of a shoe ought not to be subject to the
position of the nail-holes, but that these should be properly
placed so that fitting be guided only by the requirements
of the foot.

Each nail-hole when properly placed—neither too coarse
nor too fine—should be punched straight through the shoe and
not inclined either inwards or outwards, except at the toe
where the slope of the wall is followed by slightly pitching in.

When a fuller is used the groove made should be wide; then the farrier has more command over the direction of his nail. If the nail-hole be pitched in, the nail must take that direction and is liable to wound the foot. If the nail-hole be pitched out, the nail is prevented from taking sufficient hold of the horn.

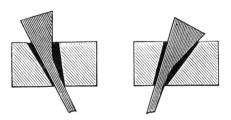

Fig. 43.—Nail-holes " pitched " in and out.

The position and direction of the nail-hole control the passage of a nail through a shoe and into the hoof. The man who drives a nail is usually blamed for laming a horse, but in most cases it would be more just to blame the man who made the nail-holes or fitted the shoe and so rendered safe driving difficult or impossible.

Each nail-hole should be as far as possible from the other— say, from an inch to an inch and a half apart   When the two front or toe nail-holes are put too far back the whole are crowded, or the last are pushed back too near the heels.

For small shoes four or five nail-holes are sufficient. Medium-sized shoes should have from five to seven, and the heavy shoes of big draught horses must have eight. The number of nail-holes need not always be increased in proportion to the size of the shoe, because as the weight of shoe is increased so is the size of the nail, and an extra strong nail may take the place of additional ones. The fewer nails in a foot the better, but as a properly-placed nail does no harm, and as the loss of a shoe may be very serious, it is better to have one too many than one too few.

Machine-made Shoes.   Horse-shoeing is distinctly an art requiring special skill for its proper performance. It is also one of the most laborious of all skilled trades. Anything which lightens mechanical toil tends to improve the mental and artistic qualities of the workman, and all applications of machinery which lessen the heavy manual labour of the farrier may therefore be looked upon as improvements.   Machinery has lightened the labour of shoe-making in two ways—by supplying various patterns of grooved and bevelled iron in bars, which only require cutting into lengths and turning round to form a shoe, and also by making shoes all ready to be fitted to the foot.   Machinery

Fig. 44.—Machine-made Shoe—Fore-foot

has not yet turned out a shoe as good and durable and well finished as the best workman can produce by hand, but it can produce many forms of shoes as good for all practical purposes, and it has this advantage—all are alike.   Bad workmen make bad shoes, but a machine, once able to produce a good model, can repeat it exactly, therefore machine-made shoes of a proper pattern are superior to all but the very best

Fig. 45.—Machine-made Shoe—Hind-foot.

hand-made shoes.   Economy, of course, is on the side of the
article produced by machinery, and all large firms keeping
their own farriers find a great saving by buying the ready-
made shoes.   Under conditions when shoes must be fitted
without a fire, as in coal mines, or in the case of armies during
a campaign, the machine-made article has the advantages of
regularity of form and a true level bearing surface.

Fig. 46.—Sections of rolled bar iron.

In little shops where often only one man is at work, either
machine-made shoes or prepared bar iron offer great con-
veniences.   The prepared bars can be bought seated on the
foot-surface and with a single or double groove on the
ground - surface.   Very narrow bars suitable for tips,
" Charlier," or light hack shoes are now widely used, and a

Fig. 47.—Sections of light pattern bar iron.

special bar—flat on the foot-surface, concave to the ground—
can be obtained which only requires cutting into lengths and
turning round to form a first-class hunting-shoe
Both prepared bars and machine-made shoes must be
judged by their form and by the material used in their
manufacture.   Some are better than others, but all have to
contend with a large amount of trade prejudice which has
little basis except in the matter of the hind shoes—here
machinery has not yet reached perfection.

CHAPTER V.

SELECTION OF SHOES.

In practice, a farrier does not trouble much about the selection of suitable shoes. The rule is to apply whatever form of shoe the horse has been wearing, and only to venture an opinion as to alterations when asked by the owner. When the selection of a suitable shoe is left to the workman he takes into consideration the work required of the horse, the form of the feet, and the wear of the old shoes. The form of the old shoes indicates not only whether a horse is a light or hard wearer but what parts of the shoe are most worn, and thus enables provision to be made against excessive or irregular wear. The form of the feet indicates not only what size of shoe is requisite but also what special weakness or strength is to be encountered. It is also necessary to note the condition of the fetlocks and knees, which may show signs of "brushing" or "speedy cutting." According to all these appearances a shoe should be selected. For the different classes of horse there are well-known forms of shoe which present special advantages, thus :-

The race horse when in training, may be shod with a very light shoe, but on the turf he requires the lightest contrivance capable of protecting the hoof and affording good foot-hold. The ordinary racing plate answers these requirements. It is made in a "crease," or tool, or may be made from specially prepared bars which only need cutting into lengths and turning round. The plate is about one-third of an inch wide by one-eighth thick. The foot-surface is flat, and the ground-surface is fullered and concave

Steeplechase plates are made on the same pattern, but should be a little stronger so as to avoid even the possibility of becoming twisted on the foot.

Hunting shoes should be light, very secure, and of a form to give good foot hold. The best are flat on the foot-surface, and fullered and concave on the ground-surface. The hind shoe should also be concave on the ground surface, but to avoid the injury of over-reaching the inner circumference at the toe should be rounded and smooth. A small square calkin at each heel affords grip on grass, and especially in going down hill at a fast pace.

Hacks, being used on hard roads, must have heavier shoes than hunters, but the form may be the same.

Carriage horses require more substance in their shoes than hacks, and the narrow concave shoes suitable for hunters and hacks cannot give sufficient durability. The double-grooved shoe known as "Rodway's" is the best for this class. On ordinary roads the hind feet may be shod with a common two heeled shoe, but on wood and asphalte the heavier sizes of Rodway iron make a shoe that affords very good foot hold and dispenses with the necessity for calkins.

Omnibus and Van horses require stronger shoes to meet the hard wear entailed by their work. The heavy Rodway iron makes very suitable front shoes, but the hind shoes must be solid with only a fullering for the nails or, as many prefer, each nail-hole separately stamped. As a rule the hind shoes of this class of horse have calkins on the outside heel. If the vehicle in which they run is provided with a foot-break calkins are unnecessary, and the advantages of a level shoe should be made use of. The advantages are— better foot hold, longer wear and less danger from treads and "cutting"

Heavy draught horses. In Scotland and in the North of England this class of horse is shod with a toe-piece and calkins on both fore and hind shoes. In London calkins are only put on the hind shoes, and toe-pieces are not used at all. On paved streets where a space exists between the rows of stones and especially if the road be hilly, I think toe-pieces are advisable, and of course when they are used calkins must be also made. Horses having become accustomed to toe-pieces, when shod with a level shoe, slip much more for a week or two than do horses which have never learned to rely upon the bar across the toe. Every thing considered, I incline to prefer a level shoe in front, and a shoe with two low square calkins behind for heavy draught horses. The enormous width of shoe often used in London is quite unnecessary, it is very heavy and it favours slipping. A narrower shoe must of course be a little thicker to meet the wear, but it is lighter and affords better foot hold, and as slipping and fatigue are both causes of excessive wear, a narrow shoe, weight for weight, will last longer than a broad flat one.

CHAPTER VI.

FITTING AND APPLICATION OF SHOES.

Having selected shoes suitable for the feet and adapted to the special work of the hoise. having also prepared the foot for shoeing, we arrive at another important part of the farriers' art—fitting the shoe. No matter what form of shoe be used or how the foot be prepared for it, unless the two are properly fitted the horse does not obtain all the advantages of good shoeing, and may be positively injured. The owner of horses seldom knows anything about the fitting of shoes, and therefore fails to appreciate how some of his directions concerning feet and shoes are quite impracticable.

I have in a previous chapter attempted to show how a foot should be prepared for shoeing, and what bearing surface should be left for the shoe. I have also described what I consider the best forms of shoe. The object at all times should be to follow nature as closely as possible, but it often happens that we may, with benefit, depart from the exact indications given and still fulfil all essential requirements. If we examine the unshod foot which has been worn down to proper proportions we find the bearing surface is not level—it is worn more at the toe and heels than elsewhere. If we

Fig. 48.

examine the ground surface of an old shoe the same thing is noticed—the surface is not level, the toe and heel show most wear. The question then arises, should we make the artificial bearing surface of the foot on the same plan and adjust the shoe to it, as in Fig. 48, or should we make the surface level and apply a level shoe as in Fig. 49.? I believe

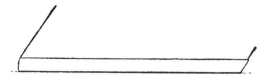

Fig. 49.

that the ideal arrangement would be to follow the line
suggested by a worn foot or a worn shoe, but it is difficult
to carry out, and greater exactness of fit is more readily
obtained by two level surfaces The ground surface of a
shoe may, if necessary, be altered to suit the outline of wear,
whilst the level foot-surface is preserved, as in Fig. 50.

Fig. 50.

Whatever form the farrier adopts, a shoe should rest equally
throughout, and the contact of foot and shoe should be exact
over the whole bearing surface. Assuming then that a properly
prepared foot presents a level surface, the fitting of shoes becomes simple so long as the smith possesses manual dexterity
and follows the indications of common sense.

There are two conditions to be fulfilled, (1) to fit the shoe
to the plain surface of the foot, (2) to fit the shoe to the circumference of the wall. Most amateurs judge shoeing by
the way a shoe follows the outline of the hoof, but the practical man knows that it is equally difficult and important to
fit the surface.

Outline fitting. A shoe is first compared with the foot, it
is then heated, and the heels cut off or turned down to the proper
length. Each limb of the shoe is fitted to follow the outline of
the wall, and it is necessary to warn the novice that the inside
and outside borders of a foot are not alike. The outside is
rounder and fuller, and the shoe should be shaped to follow
exactly the direction of the wall. The outer border of a shoe
should always be as prominent as the outer border of the
hoof; it should never be within it. The inner border must
not protrude beyond the wall lest the opposite leg be struck.

A well fitted shoe must be fitted full to the foot. What is called " close " fitting, *i.e.*, bringing the shoe rather within the circumference of the wall, is injurious, as it loses the best and strongest bearing of the wall, and permits the farrier to give an appearance of neatness by rasping away any horn which protrudes beyond the shoe On a well-shaped foot the shoe should follow the outer line of the hoof from toe to heel, but where the heels of a foot are turned inwards there is an advantage in fitting the shoe wider at the heels, as by so doing the base of the foot is not constricted and a wider resting surface is afforded to the limb When a shoe is fitted wide at the heels it is essential that the foot-surface of the shoe should be level at the heels. If it be inclined, as it often is in seated shoes, a very grave defect in the fitting results, for the heels have no level bearing-surface.

A shoe fitted too wide is liable to be trodden off by the opposite foot, or it may cause the horse to hit the opposite fetlock joint.

Provided the nail holes are properly placed, when the outside border of the shoe is fitted nicely to the circumference of the hoof, they are brought to their right position. When nail holes are placed too near, or too far, from the outer border of the shoe—*i.e*, when they are too " fine " or too "coarse"—it may be necessary to correct their position by fitting the shoe "closer" or " fuller," as the case may be. When a farrier fits shoes made by another man he may overlook this, as we are all slaves to habit. The man who in his daily practice combines "close" fitting with "fine" nailing has to alter his routine when fitting a shoe with coarse nail holes.

The length of a shoe at the heels is a matter of more importance than is generally recognised. As a rule hunters are all shod too short, while most cart horses are shod too long. The objections to a long front shoe are that it is liable to be trodden off by the hind shoe, and that it may injure the elbow when the horse lies down. A long hind shoe is free from both these disadvantages, and as it usually has a calkin is the best form to adopt.

In fitting the heels of front shoes, in all but galloping horses, the iron should generally extend slightly behind the extremity of the horn. (Fig. 48.) Horses used for galloping should have the end of the shoe just within the termination of the horn, and should finish with an oblique extremity. (Fig. 49.)

Fig. 49.—Shoe fitted short at the heels.

There is nothing gained by greater shortening, if the iron be fitted exactly to the horn. Why shoes are often pulled off, when only just the length of the hoof, is because they are not fitted close enough, and very often because they are wilfully and ignorantly designed to leave a space between hoof and iron. This so-called " eased " heel is an unmitigated evil.

Surface-fitting. It is simple to direct that the bearing-surface of a shoe should be exactly adapted to the bearing-surface of a foot. It is not so simple to carry out. When the horn on the lower surface of a foot is thin any uneven pressure —*i e.*, pressure applied directly to one spot—soon causes injury, pain, and lameness. When a good thick layer of horn exists, uneven pressures are less injurious, because the horn distributes them over a wide surface. Good workmanship is displayed by leaving no uneven pressure, and by so fitting a shoe that it shall do no harm. With a narrow shoe—one only the width of the wall—no uneven pressure can be applied to the sensitive foot, but such a shoe is seldom used as it is too light to afford sufficient wear. A wide shoe with a flat foot surface is easily fitted on all concave feet— *i.e.*, on all hind and most fore feet. To make use of the whole bearing-surface a shoe must rest evenly from toe to heel—the flat surface of the shoe must take a level bearing on the whole flat bearing-surface of the foot.

There are two places where injury from uneven pressure is most likely to happen—at the toe and at the heels.

In preparing a foot the wall at the toe may, from want of care, be reduced a little below the level of the sole, or in making a shoe the inside border at the toe may be left higher than the outside. In each case uneven pressure is placed on the sole just where the back border of the shoe rests. In fitting a hot shoe, wherever the hoof is unduly marked warning is given that pressure at that point must be prevented by altering the surface either of the shoe or the foot. On a strong foot, the knife may be used to remove a little horn ; on a weak foot the alteration must be on the shoe.

At the the heel uneven pressure is most frequent on the angle of sole between the wall and bar, where it causes the so-called "corn"—a condition in the horse having no analogy to the affliction similarly named in the human subject. It is simply a bruise of the sensitive parts under the horn.

A bruised heel—a corn—is most likely to arise from the use of a shoe too short, especially if fitted too close. It may arise from a properly-fitted shoe retained too long on the foot and shifted from its proper bearing on the wall to an improper bearing on the sole. A bruised heel may also result from the use of a well-made shoe if the preparation of the hoof has been faulty. Rule-of-thumb directions to "reduce the heels to a level by the use of the rasp, but on no account cut away any sole" may result in injury. In a strong foot with an overgrown sole it is easy to get a level surface and to fit on to it a level shoe, but the horn of the sole does not remain level. As it grows and flakes off the portion between the bar and wall is raised. If the weather be wet it swells, and then, bound down by the shoe, it acts simply as a stone might and bruises the sensitive parts within by its uneven pressure. It is always safe and it is never injurious to remove so much of the surface of this portion of sole with the drawing-knife as will ensure no uneven pressure on it by the shoe.

The more exactly the shoe fits the foot-surface the more easily it is retained in position by the nails, and the less likelihood there is of any part of it pressing distinctly on a limited portion of horn. Exact fitting allows all bearings and pressures to be distributed equally over the surface of the hoof, and thus permits the shoe most nearly to resemble a mere continuation of the hoof in iron—an arrangement to prevent wear, but not to interfere with natural functions. There is one departure from level fitting which requires special notice since it is made, not by accident or negligence, but by design. It consists in taking the bearing of an inch or an inch and a half of the extremity of a shoe off the foot. (Fig. 50.) It has been called "easing the heels," and the

Fig. 50.—An "eased" heel.

space permits a knife-blade, sometimes even a pencil, to be placed between the shoe and the foot. It is one of the very worst practices that theory has forced into horse-shoeing. Men who do it say "the heels won't stand pressure." I reply they will stand all proper pressure, and a good deal more than the quarters. But the practice does not relieve the heels of pressure. If you examine a shoe fitted in this way, after it has done a month's service, you will find it sometimes polished bright, sometimes with a deep groove worn into it. You may also test its bearing by raising the foot from the ground and inserting between shoe and hoof a flat bit of wood, then on releasing the foot and raising the opposite one, you will find that the bearing is such that the bit of wood cannot be removed. The "eased heel" does not relieve the heels of pressure but, instead of constant normal bearing, it permits a downward movement of the back of the foot at each step—which is unnatural, and which cannot occur in an unshod foot on a level surface. The "eased heel" does more than this. It wastes a large extent of good bearing surface, and it concentrates pressure at one point—where the shoe and foot meet—at the quarters. It loses good bearing-surface where it is important to have it, and unevenly throws extra weight on the quarters which are the weakest parts of the wall. An "eased heel" has not one single advantage, but it has every disadvantage which misplaced ingenuity could contrive.

For flat feet a wide shoe with a flat foot-surface is unsafe as there is liability to uneven pressure on the sole. For such feet the safer form of foot-surface is one presenting a level narrow bearing-surface round its outer border, from which an inclined or bevelled surface continues the shoe

Fig. 51.—Section of a seated shoe.

inwards. (Fig. 51) This form of shoe can be fitted to nearly any kind of foot. To escape injury to a flat sole "seating out" shoes is necessary, but the operation should always leave a level bearing-surface for the wall. When a shoe is seated from one side to the other so as to produce a saucer shaped surface harm is done to the foot. Such a shoe presents no level bearing-surface, and the weight of the horse pressing the wall on an inclined plane causes the foot to be pinched or compressed in a manner which soon causes lameness. (Fig. 52.) A few years ago these shoes were too common, and to make them still more injurious, the foot was pared out from the centre to the circumference like a saucer, and the two spoiled articles were fitted together. Their surfaces of contact were two narrow ridges which even the most expert workman could not fit without injury to the horse.

Fig. 52.—Section of a "saucer" shoe.

In Fig. 52 a shoe with an inclined surface is applied to a foot with a bearing-surface as wide as the wall but the only contact is at the edges. The horn at the edge will yield, and the hoof be pressed inwards as the weight of the animal forces the foot into the saucer-shaped shoe. When the bearing-surface of the foot, instead of being as wide as the wall, is only a ridge, the horn yields more rapidly, the clinches rise and the shoe becomes loose.

In Fig. 53 is shewn a section of another shoe with an inclined instead of a level surface, but the slope is from within outwards. The effect of this is exactly the opposite of the previous shoe. The wall is forced outwards, and if it does not as a whole yield to the pressure the portion in contact is broken. When this form of bearing-surface is adopted at the heels of a shoe the two sides of the hoof are violently forced apart, and it has even been recommended as a means of expanding the foot ; but forcible expansion is both unnecessary and dangerous.

Always regarding the shoe as an extension of the natural hoof in a harder and more durable material, it is evident that the most stability will be attained by the use of as wide a bearing surface of foot and shoe as is compatible with ease and safety to the horse.

In Fig. 54. is shown a section of a narrow shoe which takes a bearing over the whole extent of its foot-surface.

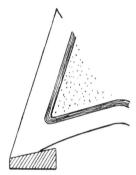

Fig. 53.—Bearing-surface inclined
outwards.

Fig. 54.—Narrow shoe with
level bearing-surface.

In Fig. 55 is shown a shoe with as wide a bearing-surface as in Fig. 54., but which loses half its bearing because the foot-surface is too narrow to utilise it.

In Fig. 56 we have a model bearing-surface on the foot, nearly twice the width of the wall, and we have a shoe with

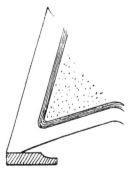

Fig. 55.—Bearing-surface of
foot too narrow.

Fig. 56.— A good bearing-
surface.

a flat foot-surface capable of using the whole bearing. Such is the fitting of all hind shoes, and it might well be adopted with advantage in all fore shoes on good feet.

Clips are thin projections drawn up from the outer border of shoes for the purpose of giving greater security to their position on a foot. On heavy cart horses the clips are some-times of great size and encourage the idea that the smith looks upon them as designed to assist the nails to retain the shoe on the foot. They should have no such purpose, their use being merely to prevent the shoe shifting to one side. A clip should not be narrow and high, it should be low and wide so that its bearing is taken against the lower edge of the wall. A high clip is a most serious danger when shoes get loose and are trodden on by the horse. The usual position for a clip is at the toe, but there are occasions when two clips— one at each side of the toe—are used. On some shoes a clip is placed at the outer quarter to prevent the shoe being dis-placed inwards; this is more often required on hind shoes. A clip at the toe affords some assistance in fitting a shoe exactly, and it also affords steadiness to the shoe during the driving of the first nails. In America clips are not used, and when American machine-made shoes were first introduced into London they were fitted without clips. I am bound to confess that these shoes did not shift on the feet to any noticeable extent, but they are now all fitted with clips so I suppose the workmen found they were an advantage. The greatest evil resulting from clips is seen in slovenly fitting, when the farrier with his knife carves out a great hole in the wall in which to imbed the clip. As a clip is flat it cannot be fitted to the rounded face of the wall, but all that is necessary is to reduce the round to a flat surface with the rasp, so that the clip may rest on it, care being taken that at the extreme edge the horn is not left so prominent as to be unduly pressed upon when the clip is driven close to the wall. It is easy to lame a horse by violently hammering up the clip, especially when the horn behind it has been so much cut away as to leave only a thin protecting layer. A clip should only be hammered up sufficiently to leave it firmly applied to the wall. A bad workman in making his clip may spoil the foot-surface of a shoe by causing a bridge on the bearing surface of the iron at the toe, and this, on thin or flat feet, may cause lameness.

A very unsightly appearance and very defective work results from the fireman leaving his clip at right angles to

the line of the shoe. It should be inclined backwards at
about the same slope as the portion of wall against which it
is to rest. The two diagrams (Fig. 57) illustrate what is
meant.

Fig. 57.—Toe Clips.

Hot and Cold Fitting. When an engineer or a car-
penter has two surfaces to fit together with great exactness
he employs some colouring material to show where they do
come in contact and where they do not. When a farrier fits a
shoe to a horse's foot he tests its adaptation by applying it
at a dull red heat to the horn. This proceeding shows
with precision the bearing surfaces, as the horn is charred
in proportion to the contact. If the shoe be found not to fit
exactly, it is taken back to the anvil and altered. It is then
again for a few seconds applied to the horn and the surface of
contact examined. This proceeding is repeated until sufficient exactness is arrived at and then the shoe is cooled ready
for nailing on. As horn is a bad conductor of heat this pro-
cess of " hot-fitting " does no harm to the sensitive structures
within the hoof unless it be carried to an extreme. When
the horn is very thin the heat of a shoe retained too long in
contact with it does serious mischief, and the injury known
as a burnt sole has often resulted from careless work. If a
shoe, whilst being altered to fit a foot, were cooled each time
it was laid on the hoof, it would have to be re-heated before
the necessary alterations could be made and this would cause
great waste of time. The abuse of hot-fitting may do harm
without any direct burning of the sole. An ill-fitting hot
shoe may be held on the hoof until it beds itself into the
horn and thus a complete correspondence between the surface
of the foot and the surface of the shoe be effected. Such a
proceeding is well described as " fitting the foot to the shoe "
and is not only destructive to the horn but damaging to the
foot by permitting an uneven shoe to look as though it were
properly fitting. When hot-fitting is used and not abused—
when it is adopted merely to indicate how and where the
shoe fits, and not to make it appear to fit—I consider it has
many advantages over cold-fitting. With some feet and

some shoes it is quite possitbe to produce a good fit without heating the shoe.   When a shoe requires much alteration to bring it into exact correspondence with the foot, even the most expert farrier cannot do justice to his work with cold iron—he gets as near to a fit as he can and when the hoof is strong little harm is done.   The best work is that which includes the greatest exactness of fit, and uneven pressure or loose shoes result from inferior work.   A badly fitted shoe requires more nails to retain it in place, and experience has shown that hot-fitted shoes give a smaller average of loose or lost shoes than those cold-fitted.   The slight charring of the end of the horn fibres which results from proper hot-fitting has never been found to do injury, and it apparently has some advantages.   One is that the surface of the hoof less readily absorbs moisture than when not charred. Another is that the horn is softened for a time and expanded, allowing nails to be easily driven, and then contracting and retaining them more firmly   The objection to hot-fitting applies only to its abuse.   The advantages are greater exactness of fit, greater security that the shoe will be firmly retained on the foot, and greater facility in the operation of shoeing.   Per-haps I ought to add that when cold-fitting is inevitable machine-made shoes are the best, because they are more regular in form, and more often level on the foot-surface than hand-made shoes.   Army studs on active service, and studs used in coal mines comprise, perhaps, the only animals upon which cold-fitting is unavoidable.

Tips are short shoes protecting only the foremost half

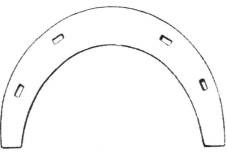

Fig. 58.

of the foot.   Upon grass or soft roads tips are quite suffi-cient to prevent undue wear of the hoof.   Even upon hard roads tips will protect the hoof in dry weather, but in wet seasons the horn becomes softened, and then that part coming in contact with hard road-surfaces wears rapidly and lameness may follow. Tips require more care in use than shoes be·cause they protect from wear only the toe, and when retained on the foot too long a time cause the hoof to become very disproportionately long at the toe. In fitting a tip care must be taken to afford the horse a level surface to bear on. The unprotected horn at the back of the foot must take a bearing on the ground level with the ground-surface of the tip. If there is sufficient horn on the foot this can be easily effected by only removing the overgrown wall to just the length the

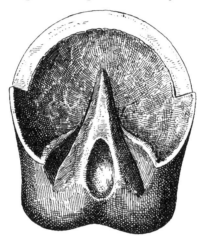

Fig. 59.—Foot prepared for a tip.

tip extends and leaving the horn behind untouched. Where there is not sufficient superfluous horn this method cannot be used, and we apply a tip gradually thinned off towards its hinder extremities. If a little horn can be removed obliquely from the front half of the foot by a few strokes of the rasp this "thinned" tip is more easily fitted so as to get a level

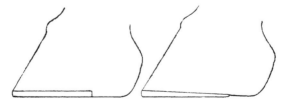

Fig. 60.—An ordinary and a "thinned" tip.

surface on the ground. When a horse has worn this form for a month it is generally possible to bring a tip, of even thickness throughout, into the same line of bearing as the horn at the heels.

Tips do not give a good foot-hold on grass, but they afford greater security of tread on hard smooth roads and on ice than long shoes. The great advantages of tips are two-fold— they are light, and they permit the greatest freedom of movement and action in the posterior part of the foot. In some cases of chronic foot lameness the use of tips and regular work will effect soundness when every other method of treatment has failed.

The Charlier System is a method of shoeing which a few years ago took a very prominent hold on the fancy of horse-owners. Like every other system it has advantages and disadvantages—it has prejudiced enemies and indiscreet friends. The principle or theory upon which it is based may be thus stated. The lower border of the wall is, it is said, the chief sustaining structure of the hoof, and as all that is required of a shoe is to prevent undue wear, therefore,

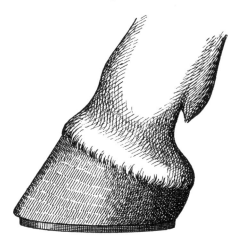

Fig. 61.—Groove for Charlier shoe formed by cutting away strip of wall.

remove a small strip of the lower border of the wall and substitute for it a similar sized strip of iron, and we shall protect from wear at the same time that we leave entirely to nature every other part of the hoof—sole, frog, and bars. This seems eminently simple and logical, but it is easy to show that it is more plausible than true. First, I would point out that the wall *only* is not the natural sustaining structure of the hoof. The wall *and the sole at its connection with the wall* is. Next I deny that the Charlier system does "leave entirely to nature every other part of the hoof." In cutting away the wall from the sole to affix the shoe, the natural function of the sole is

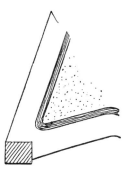

Fig. 62.—Section of Charlier shoe on foot.

seriously interfered with, and the bearing on the wall which ought to be partially distributed over the arch of the sole is limited to the wall. It is claimed that when the foot has had time to grow the sole will be found on a level with the shoe, and thus directly sharing in the weight sustaining function. I have examined many feet shod by Charlier specialists, and have never yet seen the sole of a hind foot level with the shoe three days after the shoeing. Only once have I seen the sole of the fore foot level with the shoe after a week's wear. I am often apologetically told, "Well, it is not quite in wear, but it is not an eight of an inch below the surface of the shoe." Quite so, it is *nearly* in wear, but if not actually in wear what becomes of the principle? The sole is not directly in wear and bearing is confined to the wall. As to the frog, the Charlier affords no greater use to it than any other shoe of a similar thickness, unless instead of being placed on sound firm horn it be dangerously let down into the hoof so that its edge approaches very closely to the sensitive foot. It is sometimes difficult to arrive at the truth as to the signifiance of the phrase "embedding or letting down" the shoe of the Charlier system. At one time we are assured that "the shoe is not sunk, the sole is permitted to grow up." When this is so, very little positive objection to the system can be taken, because the shoe then rests at the same level on firm horn as does any other narrow shoe ; but then the frog takes no better bearing than in other systems and the superfluous growth of horn on the sole is of no value. When the shoe is really "let down" of course the frog does receive increased pressure—it is forced to share with the wall the primary function of sustaining weight instead of, as in nature, taking only a secondary share of such action. It does this at the expense of a shoe placed so close to the "quick" that if the upper and inner border of iron be not bevelled off, immediate lameness results When the Charlier shoe was first introduced it was applied the full length of the foot, but it was found that when thinned by wear the heels spread and led to injury of the opposite leg or to its being trodden off.

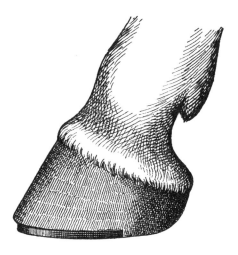

Fig. 63.—Groove for modified or short Charlier.

Now the Charlier is only applied like a tip round the front portion of the surface of the foot, and it therefore partakes of some of the advantages I have credited to tips. It is a very light shoe and only requires small nails to fix it securely, but as the shoe is only the width of the wall the nails have to be driven solely in the wall, and their position is open to the objection applying to all too fine nailing.   The disadvantages of the Charlier are its being "let down" too near the quick, its limited bearing, and its fine nail holes; the advantages are the lightness and the freedom given to the back of the foot, both of which are attainable with a narrow tip not let

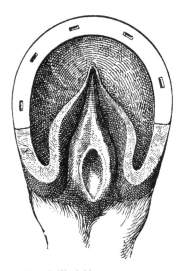

Fig 64.—A Tip laid on, not let down.

down.   One very apparent effect resulting from the use of the Charlier system is the alteration in the action of the horse. All knee action is lost, and some horses go decidedly tender whilst others acquire a low shooting stride, which is certainly not in accordance with our notions of good free locomotion.

CHAPTER VII.

"ROUGHING."

In winter, ice, snow, and frost, render roads slippery, and it is necessary to provide some arrangement whereby horses may have the greatest security of foot-hold. In countries such as Canada or Russia, where a regular winter sets in at a tolerably uniform date and continues without intermission for some months, it is easier to adopt a good system of "roughing" than in Great Britain. There, on a thick layer of ice or snow, sharp projections on the shoes cut into the surface and afford foot-hold. The edge of the projections is not soon blunted, and when once properly placed their duration is as long as the time desirable for retaining the shoe. Here, very different conditions obtain. Sometimes a week or two of frost and snow may prevail, but more frequently the spells of wintry weather are counted by days. Two or three days of frost and then two or three days of mud and slush, to be followed by either dry hard roads or a return of ice and snow, is our usual winter. We require during this time to provide for occasional days, or more rarely for weeks, of frost-bound roads. Our horses' shoes wear about a month and then require replacing by new ones. When roads are hard and dry we want no sharp ridges or points about our horses shoes, and yet we must always be able at twenty-four hours notice to supply some temporary arrangement which will ensure foot-hold.

The necessity for "roughing" and the evil effects of continuing to work unroughed horses on slippery frost-bound roads is demonstrated in London every winter by a very significant fact. If after three days of ice and snow, anyone will visit a horse-slaughterers' yard, he will find the place full of dead horses which have fallen in the streets and suffered incurable or fatal injury. A sudden and severe attack of ice and snow half paralyses the horse traffic of a large town for a day or two, and many owners will sooner keep their horses in the stable than go to the expense of having them roughed. The loss in civil life from unpreparedness for ice and snow is very serious, but the loss which has fallen upon military movements from similar neglect is appalling. Napoleon's rout from Moscow in 1814, Bourbaki's flight into Switzerland in 1871, and the Danish retreat upon Koenigsgratz in 1865 are terrible instances of the frightful loss sustained when horses are unable to keep on their feet at a walk, let alone drag guns and wagons over an ice-covered surface.

A well-managed stud of horses which is required to face all weather and to work every day through an English winter should, from December 1st to March 1st, be shod in such a manner as to be easily and speedily provided with mechanism which will afford secure foot-hold. This may be effected by the use of moveable steel "roughs" or "sharps." Of course the cost is the argument against them, but this should be considered in view of the probability or certainty of loss which will follow from neglect. If we allow common humanity to animals to enter into the consideration, economy will be served by adopting a well arranged system of roughing. Every good horseman appreciates the enormity of over-loading, but neglect of roughing causes just as much cruelty. A horse that on a good road can properly draw a

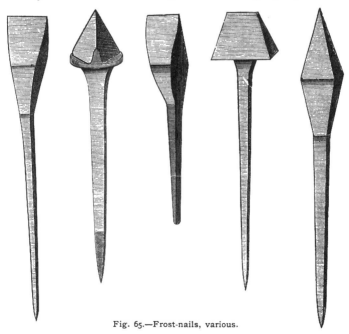

Fig. 65.—Frost-nails, various.

ton would be considered over-loaded with two tons, and his struggles to progress would at once attract attention. The same animal with half a ton on an ice-covered surface would suffer more exhaustion, fatigue, and fright, and run more risk of fatal injury than in the case of the over-loading, but his owner who would indignantly repudiate the one condition will designedly incur the other.

Probably this is only thoughtlessness, but it is a reflection on the prudence of a manager, and certainly not flattering to the feelings or intelligence of a man.

There are many ways of providing foot-hold for a horse on ice and snow. The most simple and temporary proceeding is to use frost-nails. Fig. 65 shows various sizes and shapes of these articles.

They are not driven through the hoof like ordinary nails, but through the shoe only, which is prepared for their reception at the time of fitting. A shoe to carry frost-nails is fitted a little wider than usual at the heels and has at its extremities, or more often at its outer extremities, countersunk holes stamped and directed outwards so that the frost-nail can be safely driven through by anyone and its shank turned down over the shoe. There is a difficulty in firmly securing them, they are apt to work loose and then become bent and useless. If used on the inside heel of a shoe they constitute a danger to the opposite leg should they bend and protrude from under the shoe. As a temporary provision against a sudden frost or fall of snow they are useful—but they are only a make-shift.

The more permanent and effective system of " roughing " consists in removing the shoes and turning down a sharp chisel projection at the heels. In very bad weather a projecting edge is also laid across the toe of the shoe.

The diagrams show the method of "sharping" a front and hind shoe at the heels only. The hind shoe, having calkins,

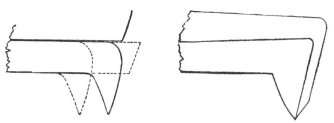

Fig. 66.—Heels of Fore and Hind Shoes, sharped.

is not much altered. The smith simply converts the square calkin into a sharp-edged one. The fore shoe having no calkins is turned down at the heels to afford enough iron to form the 'sharp.' But this shortens the shoe, and if it be repeated two or three times, as it often is, the bearing surface is spoiled, and the slightest carelessness in fitting the shoe causes a bruised heel. 'Roughing' is generally done in a hurry. A dozen horses reach the farrier's shop at one time and all desire to return to work with as little delay as possible. The work is perforce hurried through, careful fitting cannot be done, and bad-footed horses suffer accordingly. The dotted lines in Fig. 66 show the original length of shoe, and the shortening which results from a second roughing.

All horse-owners know how many lame horses result from the repeated roughings necessitated by a week or two of wintry weather. Some of this is inevitable from the rush and hurry which cannot be prevented. Valuable horses with weak feet should not be submitted to any such risk. They should be shod with removable sharps. The mere fact of removing a horse's shoes perhaps five or six times in a month must injure the hoof. Add to this the shortening of the shoe, the raising of the heel by the roughing, and the irregular bearing due to hurried fitting and we have conditions which only the very strongest feet can endure without serious injury.

For heavy draught horses, and for all where the roads are hilly, the toes as well as the heels must be 'sharped' when ice and snow are firm on the surface. Fig. 67 shows this arrangement at the toe. The removable steel "sharps," of which

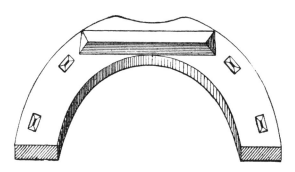

Fig. 67.—Toe Sharp.

I have spoken, are certainly the least objectionable method of providing foot-hold in winter. They are made in various sizes to suit all kinds of shoes. They vary in shape some-what, but their form is more a matter of fancy than utility.

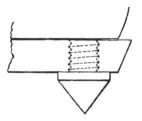

Fig. 68.—Removable Steel Sharp.

One in each heel of a shoe is the usual number used but if snow and ice are plentiful and the roads hilly two additional "sharps" may be placed at the toe of the shoe.

Fig. 69.—Steel Sharps, screw.

At the time of fitting the shoes, holes are made by first punching a round hole through the heels—and through the toe if desired—then the hole is 'tapped' and a thread formed to fit it in the shank of the sharp which is to fill it. If the sharps are not immediately wanted the holes may be filled with corks to keep out the grit and dirt. When corks are used the wear of the shoe causes a burr to form round the edge of the hole, and before the sharp can be screwed in a "tap" must be worked into each hole to clear the thread. One great objection to this method is that as the shoe wears it becomes thinner, and if much worn the shank of the "sharp" may be too long, and when screwed home cause pressure upon the hoof and consequent lameness. To guard against this steel "blanks" are used to preserve the holes, and when a frost comes they are removed and the "sharps" put in.

The blanks vary in height and of course those least in height are best for the horse's action, but they must not be allowed to get so worn that it is impossible to remove them. These blanks are shown below.

Fig. 70.—Blanks, screwed.

The "tapping" and "screwing" of shoes is expensive, and in small shops must be done by hand. In large shops a gas engine and a machine would reduce the cost very greatly, and if the system came into general use this method of providing against frost-bound roads could be carried out at much less cost than now. With a view to economy and simplicity a sharp has been invented which requires no screw.

Fig. 71.—Steel Sharps and Blank, Plug shanks.

The shank may be either round or square. A hole is punched in the heel of the shoe and carefully guaged to the size of the shank of the "sharp." The sharp is then put in and a tap of the hammer secures it. The difficulty is to get the hole in the shoe and the shank of the sharp of corresponding form and size. When this is done the sharp keeps its place and is not difficult to remove. Too often, however, they are not uniform, and then the sharp falls out or sometimes cannot be removed When the holes are drilled instead of punched the fit is more exact, but this only applies to those with a round shank. A slight taper is given both to the hole and the shank of the "sharp." As with the screw sharps so with these, blanks are used to keep the holes open until the road-surface requires the sharp.

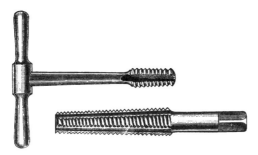

Fig. 72.—Steel Taps for screwing shoes.

No sharps should be left in shoes when the horses are stabled at night, as serious injuries to the coronet may result from a tread by the opposite foot. The coachman or horse-keeper must be supplied with a spanner to remove the screws, and with a tap to clear the holes if blanks are not used.

For roads not badly covered with snow and ice, sufficient security is afforded by some forms of india-rubber pads, which will be described in a future chapter.

CHAPTER VIII.

Injuries from Shoeing.

Even with the most careful farrier injury may occur during shoeing, or may arise as the result of the operation. Sometimes the foot, from its condition or form, renders an accident possible, and it may be so diseased, or defective, as to render shoeing with safety very improbable Sometimes the shoe is to blame, and sometimes the nail or clip. A few words about each of the common injuries may be useful as helps to their avoidance or as guides to their remedying.

From nails two kinds of injury may result. The most common arises from the nail being driven too near the sensitive parts, and is known as a *bind*. The nail does not really penetrate the sensitive foot, but is so near as to press unduly upon it. This condition causes lameness, which is generally not noticed till a day or two after the shoeing It is readily detected by the farrier on removing the shoe and trying all the tracks of the nails in the hoof by pressure with pincers. When the lameness is slight removal of the nail and one or two days rest are all that is required. When the lameness is great it may be suspected that the injury has caused the formation of matter within the hoof. This must, of course, be allowed to escaped, and the services of a veterinary surgeon are advisable.

Any neglect in these cases, such as working the horse after lameness has appeared, or delay in removing the offending nail, may lead to very serious changes in the foot, or even to death of the horse.

Another injury caused by nails is from a direct puncture of the sensitive foot. This may be slight, as in cases where the farrier in driving the nail misdirects it and so stabs the sensitive parts, but immediately withdraws the nail knowing what has happened. The lameness resulting from this is usually slight. Very much more serious is the lameness resulting from a nail which pierces the sensitive foot and is not recognised at once by the farrier. As a rule, lameness is immediate, and should the horse perform a journey before the nail is removed, serious damage is certain to follow.

Want of skill in driving a nail is not always the chief cause of "binding" or "pricking" a horse. More often than not the form and position of the nail-holes is the primary cause, for if the nail-holes in the shoe are too "coarse" or badly pitched it is quite impossible to safely drive nails through them. Sometimes the nails are defective, and this was much more common when nails were all hand-made. Bad iron or bad workmanship led to nails splitting within the hoof, and whilst one half came out through the wall the other portion turned in and penetrated the sensitive foot causing a most dangerous injury. The best brands of machine-made nails, now generally used, are remarkably free from this defect.

No lameness resulting from injury by a nail should be neglected. If detected and attended to at once few cases are serious. If neglected, the very simplest may end in permanent damage to the horse. By treating these accidents as unpardonable, horse-owners rather encourage farriers to disguise them or to not acknowledge them. If the workman would always be careful to search for injury and when he found it acknowledge the accident, many simple cases would cease to develope into serious ones Frank acknowledgement is always best, but is less likely to take place when it is followed by unqualified blame than when treated as an accident which may have been accompanied by unavoidable difficulties.

From clips lameness may arise. A badly drawn clip is not easily laid level and flat on the wall. When hammered down excessively it causes pressure on the sensitive foot, and lameness. When side clips are used—one each side of the foot—it is not difficult to cause lameness by driving them too tightly against the wall. They then hold the hoof as if in a vice. When shoes get loose or are partially torn off the horse may tread on the clip, and if it be high and sharp very dangerous wounds result.

From the shoe, injury results from any uneven pressure, especially when the horny covering of the foot is weak and thin. The horn becomes broken and split, and the bearing for a shoe is more or less spoiled. Flat feet are liable to be bruised by the pressure of the inner circumference of the shoe at the toe. Lameness from this cause is easily detected by removing the shoe and testing the hoof with the pincers. If attended to at once, and the bearing of the shoe removed from the part little injury results. If neglected, inflammatory changes in the sensitive parts are sure to arise.

Corns in horses are due to bruising of the angle of the sole by the heel of the shoe. A wide open foot with low heels is most likely to suffer, but any foot may be injured. The most common seat of injury is the inner heel of a fore-foot. Even a properly fitted shoe may cause a corn if retained too long upon a foot, as then, owing to the growth of the hoof, its extremity is carried forward from beneath the wall so as to press upon the sole. A short shoe, fitted too close on the inside, is the most common cause of corn. To guard against the shoe being trodden on by the opposite foot the inside is generally fitted close, and to guard against being trodden on by the hind foot it is often fitted short. Thus to prevent accidents of one kind methods are adopted which, being a little overdone, lead to injury of another. A not uncommon error in the preparation of the foot for shoeing may also lead to the production of the so-called corn. If the wall on the inside heel be lowered more than it should be the horn of the sole is left higher than the wall, and then a level shoe presses unevenly upon the higher part.

A corn, be it remembered, is not a tumour or a growth, it is merely a bruise of the sensitive foot under the horn of the sole. It shows itself by staining the horn red, just as a bruise on the human body shows a staining of the skin above it. To "cut out a corn" with the idea of removing it is simply an ignorant proceeding. If a corn be slight all that is necessary is to take off the pressure of the shoe, and this is assisted by removing a thin slice or two of horn at the part When the injury is very great matter may be formed under the horn, and of course must be let out by removal of the horn over it. Provided there is no reason to believe that matter has formed, a corn, *i.e.*, the bruised and discoloured horn, should not be dug out in the ruthless manner so commonly adopted. Cutting away all the horn of the sole at the heels leaves the wall without any support. When the the shoe rests upon the wall it is unable to sustain the weight without yielding, and thus an additional cause of irritation and soreness is manufactured. The excessive paring of corns is the chief reason of the difficulty of getting permanently rid of them. The simplest device for taking all pressure off a corn is to cut off an inch and a half of the inner heel of the shoe. With the three-quarter shoe (Fig. 73)

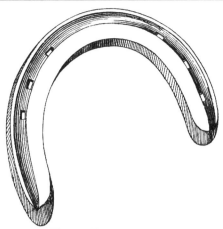

Fig. 73.—Three-quarter Shoe.

a horse will soon go sound, and his foot will then resume its healthy state. The saying "once a corn, always a corn" is not true, but it is true that a bruised heel is tender and liable to bruise again, from very slight unevenness of pressure, for at least three months. All that is necessary is care in fitting and abstention from removal of too much horn at the part. Of course when the degree of lameness is such as to suggest that matter is formed the horn must be cut away so as to afford an exit for it, but the majority of corns are detected long before the stage of suppuration has resulted from a bruise.

A burnt Sole. In fitting a hot shoe to a foot it some-times happens that the sensitive parts under the sole at the toe are injured by heat. This is most likely to occur with a foot on which the horn is thin, especially if it also be flat or convex. Burning the sole is an injury which must be put down to negligence. It does not occur from the shoe being too hot but from its being too long retained, and may be expected when the fireman is seen holding a dull-red hot shoe on to a foot, with a doormen assisting to "bed it in" by pressing it to the foot with a rasp. When the heat of a shoe penetrates through the horn with sufficent intensity to blister the sensitive parts of the foot great pain and lameness result. In many cases separation of the sole from the "quick" takes place, and some weeks pass before the horse can resume work.

Treads are injuries to the coronet caused by the shoe of the opposite foot, and are usually found on the front or inside of the hind feet. The injury may take the form of a bruise and the skin remain unbroken, it may appear as a superficial jagged wound, or it may take the form of a tolerably clean cut, in which case, although at first bleeding is very free, ultimate recovery is rapid. Bruises on the coronet—just where hair and hoof meet—are always to be looked upon as serious. The slighter cases, after a few days pain and lameness, pass away leaving only a little line showing where the hoof has separated from the skin. This separation is not serious unless a good deal of swelling has accompanied it, and even then only time is required to effect a cure. In more serious cases an extensive slough takes place, and the coronary band which secretes the wall may be damaged. The worst cases are those in which deep seated abscesses occur, as they often terminate in a " quittor." The farrier should always recognise a tread as possibly dangerous and obtain professional advice.

It is a common custom to rasp away the horn of the wall immediately beneath any injury of the coronet, but it is a useless proceeding which weakens the hoof and does no good to the inflamed tissues above or beneath.

Treads are most common in horses shod with heavy shoes and high calkins—a fact which suggests that a low square calkin and a shoe fitted not too wide at the heels is a possible preventive.

" Cutting " or " Brushing."

By these terms is meant the injury to the inside of the fetlock joint which results from bruising by the opposite foot. Possibly some small proportion of such injuries are traceable to the system of shoeing, to the form of shoe, or to the action of the horse. They are, with few exceptions, the direct result of want of condition in the horse and are almost confined to young horses, old weak horses, or animals that have been submitted to some excessively long and tiring journey. The first thing a horse-owner does when his horse "brushes" is to send him to the farrier to have his shoes altered. In half the cases there is nothing wrong with the shoes, and all that is required is a little patience till the horse gains hard condition. At the commencement of a coaching season half the horses "cut" their fetlocks, no matter how they are shod. At the end of the season none of them touch the opposite joint, with perhaps a few exceptions afflicted with defective formation of limb, or constitutions that baffle all attempts at getting hard condition. The same thing is seen in cab and omnibus stock. All the new horses "cut" their legs for a few weeks. The old ones, with a few exceptions, work in any form of shoe, but never touch their joints They "cut" when they are out of condition—when their limbs soon tire; but they never "cut" when they are in condition—when they have firm control of the action of their limbs. There are, however, a few horses that are always a source of trouble, and there are conditions of shoeing which assist or prevent the injury. The hind legs are the most frequently affected and this because of the calkins. Many horses will cease "cutting" at once if the calkins of the shoes be removed and a level shoe adopted. There are certain forms of shoe which are supposed to be specially suitable as preventives. A great favourite is the ' knocked-up-shoe "—*i.e.*, a shoe with no nails on the inside except at the toe, and a skate-shaped inner branch.

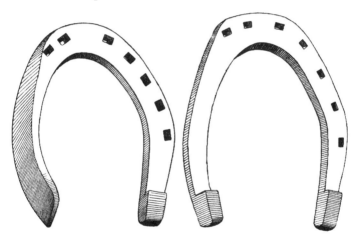

Fig. 74.—" Knocked-up " Shoes—with and without an inner Calkin.

These shoes are fitted not only close to the inner border of the wall but within it, and the horn at the toe is then rasped off level with the shoe. Whether they are of any use is a question, but there is no question of the harm they do to the foot. Some farriers are partial to a three-quarter-shoe—one from which a couple of inches of the inside heel has been removed. Some thicken the outside toe, some the inside toe. Some raise one heel, some the other, and some profess to have a principle of fitting the shoe based upon the formation of the horse's limb and the peculiarity of his action. If in practice success attended these methods I should advise their adoption, but my experience is that numerous farriers obtain a special name for shoeing horses that "cut," when their methods, applied to quite similar cases, are as antagonistic as the poles. A light shoe without calkins has at any rate negative properties—it will not assist the horse to injure himself. For all the other forms and shapes I have a profound contempt, but as people will have changes, and as the most marked departure from the ordinary seems to give the greatest satisfaction, it is perhaps "good business" to supply what is appreciated.

The two great cures for "cutting" are—regular work and good old beans. When a man drives a horse forty miles in a day at a fast pace he, of course, blames the farrier for all damage to the fetlocks. He is merely illogical.

Over-reaching.

This is an injury to the heel—generally the inner—of a front foot. The heel is struck by the inner border of the toe of the hind shoe. Over-reach occurs at a gallop in this

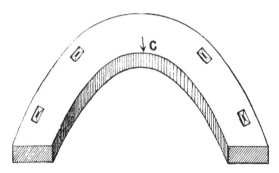

Fig. 75.—Toe of Hind Shoe showing the edge which cuts the Front Foot.

country, but is seen in America as the result of a mis-step in the fast trotters. An over-reach can only occur when the fore foot is raised from the ground and the hind foot reaches right into the hollow of the fore foot. When the fore and hind feet in this position separate the inner border of the toe of the hind shoe catches the heel of the fore foot and cuts off a slice. This cut portion often hangs as a flap, and when it does the attachment is always at the back, showing that the injury was not from behind forwards as it would be if caused by a direct blow, but from before backwards—in other words by a dragging action of the hind foot as it leaves the front one. An over-reach then may result either from the fore limb being insufficiently extended, or from the hind limb being over extended.

The prevention of this injury is effected by rounding off the inside edge of the hind shoe as shown below.

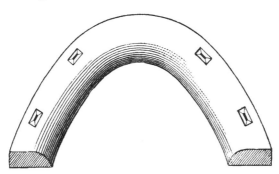

Fig. 76.—Toe of Hind Shoe showing rounded inside border.

Speedy-cut.

This is an injury inflicted on the inner surface of the lower part of the knee joint by a blow from the toe of the shoe of the opposite foot. It occurs at a trot, and very seldom except when a horse is tired or over-paced A horse that has once "speedy-cut" is apt to do so again and it may cause him to fall. Such horses should be shod "close" on the inside, and care should be taken that the heels of the foot which strikes should be kept low. In some cases a three-quarter shoe (see Fig. 73) on the offending foot prevents injury.

" Forging " or " Clacking."

This is not an injury but an annoyance. It is the noise made by the striking of the hind shoe against the front as the horse is trotting. Horses "forge" when young and green, when out of condition or tired. As a rule, a horse that makes this noise is a slovenly goer, and will cease to annoy when he gets strength and goes up to his bit. Shoeing makes a difference, and in some cases at once stops it. The part of the front shoe struck is the inner border round the toe. (Fig. 77). The part of the hind shoe that strikes is the outer border at the inside and outside toe. (Fig. 78).

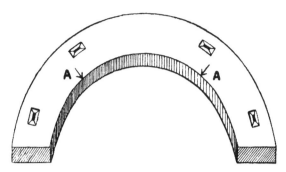

Fig. 77.—Toe of Fore Shoe.   The arrows mark the place struck in "forging."

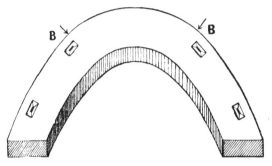

Fig. 78.—Toe of Hind Shoe showing the edge which strikes the Fore Shoe.

To alter the fore shoe, round off the inner border ; or use a shoe with no inner border such as the concave hunting shoe.

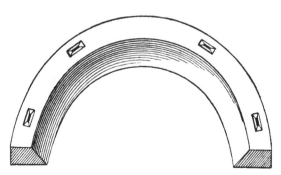

Fig. 79.—Toe of Fore Shoe with inner border bevelled off.

To alter the toe of the hind shoe is useless, but by using a level shoe without calkins some advantage is gained. A so-called "diamond-toed" shoe has been recommended. It is not advisable as it does no good except by causing its point to strike the sole of the front foot. If by such a dodge the sound is got rid of it is only by running the risk of injuring the foot.

CHAPTER IX.

SHOEING BAD FEET.

Any average farrier can shoe without immediate harm a good well-formed foot that has a thick covering of horn, but when the horn is deficient in quantity or quality injury soon takes place if a badly fitted shoe be applied. There are feet which from disease or accident or bad shoeing have become, more or less, permanently damaged. Some are seriously altered in shape. Some are protected only by an unhealthy horn, and some show definite changes which cause weakness at a special part. These are the feet which really test the art of the farrier, for he must know just what to do and what not to do, and must possess the skill to practice what he knows.

Flat Feet. Some horses are born with flat feet, others acquire them as the result of disease. Too often the flat sole has another defect accompanying it—low weak heels Such feet are best shod with a seated shoe so as to avoid any uneven pressure on the sole, and the shoes should always be fitted a little longer than the bearing-surface of the foot, so as to avoid any risk of producing a bruise at the heel—in other words, of causing a corn. The seated shoe is not advisable on a hunter. The concave shoe used for hunters has many distinct advantages and only one disadvantage for a flat foot, viz , that it has a wide flat foot-surface. It may cause an uneven pressure at the toe on a flat sole, but this is easily avoided by not making it too wide ; perhaps the very worst thing to do with a flat foot is to try and make it look less flat by paring it down. The thinner the horn the greater the chance of injury to the sensitive parts under it, and every injury tends to make the sole weaker. Leaving the sole strong and thick, whilst fitting the shoe to avoid uneven pressure, is the principle of shoeing to be adopted with flat feet.

Convex Soles. The sole of the foot should be concave, but as the result of disease many feet become convex. This bulging or "dropping" of the sole varies in degree from a little more than flat to an inch or so below the level of the wall. When the under-surface of a horse's foot resembles in form the outside of a saucer, fitting a shoe becomes a work of art. Very often the wall is brittle and broken away and it is most difficult to find sufficient bearing-surface on the foot for a shoe. Many of these feet may be safely shod with a narrow shoe that rests only on the wall and the intermediate horn between the wall and sole. Such a shoe may, according to the size of the foot, be five-eighths or even three-quarters of an inch wide. Its thickness is to be such as will prevent the sole taking any direct bearing on the ground, and sometimes a shoe of this form is much thicker than it is wide. The advantage of this shoe is that it is so narrow that any bearing on the sole is avoided. The disadvantage is that on rough roads the sole may be bruised by the flint or granite stones. When the horn of a "dropped" sole is very thin, or when the horse has to work on roads covered with sharp loose stones, some cover for the sole is necessary and the narrow shoe is not practicable. To provide cover for the sole, the web of the shoe has to be wide, and, therefore, the foot-surface of the shoe must be seated out so as to avoid contact with

Improper bearing surface. Fig. 80. A level bearing surface.

the sole. Too often the seating is continued from the inner to the outer border of a shoe, so that no level bearing-surface is provided for the wall to rest on. This kind of shoe is like the hollow of a saucer, and when applied to a foot is certain to cause lameness soon or later. Each time the horse rests his weight on it the hoof is compressed by the inclined surface of the shoe, which instead of providing a firm bearing-surface affords only an ingenious instrument of torture.

In even the worst of these deformed feet some good sound horn is to be found at the heels, where an inch or sometimes two can be utilised for level bearing. No matter how much seating is required at the toe and quarters, the heel of the shoe may always be made level.

It cannot be too strongly urged that in the preparation of feet with bulging soles no horn is to be removed from the sole. The toe is to be shortened, the heels lowered proportionately, and the bearing-surface of the wall made level with a rasp. At no place must the shoe rest on the sole. In nearly every case the toe is left too long and the bearing taken upon it by the shoe only increases the deformity. In many feet a large slice might be sawn off the toe with advantage, as the sensitive foot is separated from the wall by a mass of diseased horn which presses the wall at the toe forward. (Fig. 81).

Deformity resulting from Laminitis.   Fig. 81.   Section showing how front of wall is separated from sensitive laminæ.

Sandcracks. This is the name given to cracks in the wall which commence at the coronet and extend downwards. From their position at the toe, or at the side of the hoof, they are sometimes called respectively " toe-cracks " and "quarter-cracks." The crack may be very slight and may exist without causing lameness. It may appear suddenly, accompanied by great lameness and by the issue of blood from between the edges of the divided wall. These are grave cases which require surgical attendance. Sandcracks are most commonly seen in dry brittle feet, and the horses most subject to them are those employed in heavy draught work. Railway shunt-horses and omnibus horses are very liable to be troubled with sandcracks in the toe of the hind feet.

In shoeing for this defect there are two things to avoid, (a) not to place any direct pressure on the part; (b) not to fit a shoe which will tend to force the crack open. Following these lines it is well not to put a clip exactly over a crack. If at the toe place a clip each side of the crack, and never use calkins or high heels which throw the weight forward. If at the quarter avoid a spring-heeled shoe which permits the downward movement of the foot behind the crack and so forces it open. In all cases, after fitting the shoe level to the foot, remove a little more horn just below the crack so as to relieve the direct bearing on the part. (Fig. 82).

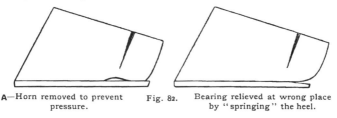

A—Horn removed to prevent   Fig. 82.   Bearing relieved at wrong place
        pressure.   by "springing" the heel.

In the case of crack extending the whole space of the wall some provision should always be made to keep it from opening, because every step of the horse, especially when drawing a load, causes an outward pressure at the coronet. This pressure forces the hoof apart and the injury caused does not cease with the pain and lameness which follow, and which may be temporary. Doubtless the original cause of a sandcrack is some morbid condition of the coronary band— the band from which the wall grows. The sensitive laminæ are at first not affected further than by the inflammation consequent upon the direct tearing which occurs when the crack takes place. The continued irritation, kept up by a persistent fissure in the horn covering the laminæ, soon causes other serious changes which tend to make the sandcrack a permanent disease. Thus even the smallest crack should be attended to and measures adopted to prevent its enlargement or, when extensive, to limit all opening and shutting movement of the hoof.

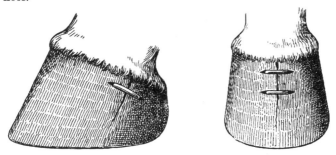

Fig. 83.—French Clips in Position.

This is sometimes attempted by a simple leather strap tightly applied, or by binding the foot with string or tape. Tape is less liable to slip than string. When the hoof is sufficiently thick two nails may be driven in opposite directions transversely through the crack and clinched; or French sand-crack-clips (Fig. 83) may be used which are easily applied. The instruments necessary are shown below (Fig. 84). The iron (*b*)

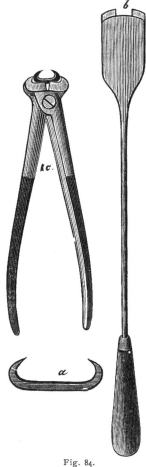

is made red-hot and pressed on the hoof over the crack so as to burn a groove each side of it. Into these grooves the clip (*a*) is put and the pincers (*c*) are then used to compress the clip firmly into its place. There is a strain upon the clips, and sometimes one breaks. It is therefore necessary always to use two, and for an extensive crack three may be employed.

All these appliances tend to keep the lips of the crack from separating, but they do not prevent the edges of a deep wide crack from being forced together and thus pinching the sensitive parts. To provide against this injury a slip of hard wood may be fitted into the crack, and then the nails or clips may be more safely drawn tight without fear of injury, and with a better chance of preventing any movement in the edges of the crack. To insert the wood, the crack is converted into a groove nearly as deep as the wall, about three-eights of an inch wide, with straight sides, or better still, with a little greater width at the bottom than at the surface. Into such a groove a piece of wood formed to fit it is gently driven from below and rasped off to fit exactly. Or, softened gutta-percha may be press-ed firmly into the space and levelled off when cold.

Fig. 84.

To "cut out" a sandcrack except for the purpose of re-filling it is bad practice as it favours movement and helps to make the defect permanent. To rasp away the horn so that only a thin layer is left is also injurious. No horn should be removed except for the fitting of a plug as above described or, under veterinary direction, for the purpose of giving vent to matter which has formed within the hoof.

In many European countries a shoe is used for toe-cracks which has two clips drawn on the inside border of the shoe at the heels. These clips catch the bars of the hoof and prevent the heels of the foot closing in. The idea is that

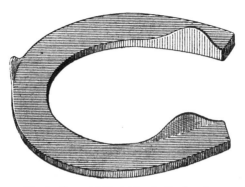

Fig. 85—Shoe with Heel Clips for Sandcrack.

when the wall at the heels contracts, there is a tendency for the wall at the toe, if separated by a crack, to open. Fig. 85 shows the position of the clips which must be carefully fitted so as to rest on the inside of the bars. Mr. Willis, V.S., has tried these shoes and speaks well of their utility.

When the crack is in the quarters of the foot, it is not the tendency to expansion of the hoof that has to be guarded against. It is the downward motion of the heels that forces open a crack in this position. The farrier provides against this by taking care to have a firm bearing of the shoe on the hoof behind the crack as shown in A figure 82.

Contracted Feet. Some diseases of the foot lead to contraction of the hoof, which is most noticeable round the coronet and at the heels Any long continued lameness which prevents the horse placing the usual weight on the foot may be accompanied by contraction. Constant cutting away of the bars and paring the frog so that it takes no contact with the ground also leads to shrinking in of the heels. By lowering the heels and letting the frog alone many feet will in time widen out to their proper size, but no system of shoeing is so good for contracted feet as the use of tips, which leave the whole back part of the hoof to take direct bearing on the ground.

Many shoes have been invented for forcing open the heels of contracted feet. Some have had a hinge at the toe and a movable screw at the heel. Some have had the bearing-surface at the heels made with a slope outwards, (See Fig. 53, page 74) so that the weight of the horse should constantly tend to force the heels apart. There is no necessity for any of these contrivances. A properly fitted tip (See page 78) will permit the hoof gradually to expand to its healthy size and form.

Seedy-toe. This is a condition of the wall usually found at the toe but not uncommon at the quarters. It is not common in hind feet but occurs sometimes. When the shoe is removed a separation is noticed between the sole and the wall, and this separation may extend up the wall nearly to the coronet. As a rule the space so formed is a narrow one, but it may be wide enough to admit three fingers of a man's hand. Probably all seedy toes result from some injury or disease of the coronary band from which the wall grows, and the first appearance is not a cavity but a changed and softened horn, which may be dry and crumbly, or moist and cheesy. The diseased horn may be scraped out and the cavity filled with tar and tow. The wall bounding the cavity should be relieved of all pressure on the shoe, and if a radical cure be desired all the un-attached wall should be cut away. This, however, should be done under veterinary guidance.

Turning in of the Wall. By this expression, I mean those cases of weak low-heels in which the border of the wall turns inward. Such a form of horn offers no suitable bearing for a shoe, and if submitted to pressure by a shoe gets worse. Too often this condition is treated by paring away the sole within, which increases the deformity. The sole should not be cut but be left as strong as possible. The curled-in border of the wall should be cut down and all bearing taken off the shoe. In one or two shoeings the wall will resume its proper form. When both heels are so affected, and the horse has to remain at work, only one heel must be treated at a time. The extreme point of the heel is never affected, and affords a point for bearing when the border of wall in front of it is cut away so as not to touch the shoe.

CHAPTER X.

LEATHER AND RUBBER PADS.

In the days when farriers were driven by theoretical teachers to pare out the soles and otherwise rob the foot of its natural covering of horn, artificial protection had frequently to be given to the foot. A horse with a thin sole could not travel over rough roads, on which sharp loose stones were plentiful, without great risk of injury ; consequently in those times plates of leather were often used to protect the foot. When a horse went " a little short " his owner not unnaturally concluded that he had bruised his foot and that the protection of a leather sole would be beneficial. In many cases the defective action was due to other cause than bruising, but still the leather was adopted, and it soon became an accepted theory that leather soles modified concussion and protected the foot from jar. This is more than doubtful, and I hold a very firm opinion that a plate of leather between the shoe and the foot has no such effect, whilst it interferes with the exactness of fit of the shoe. "Leathers" are useful on weak feet to protect a thin or defective sole from injury. When the under surface of a foot has been bruised, cut through, or when it is diseased, leather offers a useful protection, but when the sole is firm and sound it is quite unnecessary.

To apply leather properly, a square piece fully the size of the shoe is taken. A portion is then cut out where the clip has to fit and all protruding parts cut away level with the border of the shoe. If applied without more precautions, an open space would be left between leather and sole into which mud and grit would find their way and the leather would soon be cut through by resting on the irregular surface of the frog. To prevent this mischief the under surface of the foot is made level before the shoe is applied. The leveling is managed by spreading a paste of tar and oatmeal over the sole, and filling up the space at the sides of the frog with tow. Then the shoe with the leather is nailed on in the usual manner, The belief in leather as an anti-concussive appliance has led to the use of what are called " ring-leathers." These are not plates covering the whole under surface of the foot but narrow bands fixed between shoe and hoof. They are absolutely use-less, in fact their only possible effect is to spoil the fit of the shoe. Plates of india-rubber have been tried between the shoe and the foot as preventives of concussion. They invariably fail by reason of their effect upon the shoe. At each step when the weight of the horse comes on the foot the elastic rubber yields, the shoe is pressed closer to the foot, the nails are loosened, and when the foot is raised the rubber rebounds. The shoe soon becomes so loose that it is cast or torn off. Nothing elastic should be placed between shoe and foot. When an elastic or spring is applied it must be between the shoe and the ground.

Various arrangements have been adopted to supply the horse's foot with some provision against concussion. Injured and diseased feet may no doubt be benefitted by some elastic appliance which secures them from the jar of contact on a hard road. They may be protected against direct bruise. The healthy foot requires no such protection. Nature has covered it with a thick layer of horn and has provided against concussion by quite other means—by the co-ordinate action of muscles, by the oblique position of the pastern and by the construction of the back part of the foot.

Quite apart from any attempt to prevent concussion a valu-able use has been found for indiarubber pads in connection with horse-shoeing. The improvement in modern road-surfaces has been accompanied by an increased facility for slipping, and it has been found that no material gives such security of foot-hold on smooth surfaces as india-rubber.

The earliest of these contrivances with which I am ac-quainted was formed so as to leave the frog uncovered whilst a bearing of rubber was given all round the inner circum-ference of the shoe. This pad had a wide flat border which fitted under the shoe, with which it was nailed on to the foot Its great objection was that it could not be nicely fitted on many feet without first cutting away the bars.

Then we had rubber pads which were not nailed on with the shoe, but which fitted into the shoe and were removed at will. The objection to these was that they could only be used with a seated shoe and could not be applied with a narrow shoe or one possessing a flat foot-surface.

The next form to appear was a leather sole on which an artificial frog was fixed. Great difficulty was at first experienced in fixing this frog so that it remained firm. The difficulty has not yet been surmounted by all makers, but Mr. G. Urquhart, of London, makes a most reliable article. These "frog-pads" certainly give a very good foot-hold on all kinds of paved streets.

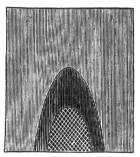

Fig. 86.—Frog-pad.

A pad of very elegant appearance is "Sheather's Pneumatic." It is not solid like the ordinary frog-pad but hollow and is compressed at each step but immediately resumes its prominent form on being relieved of pressure.

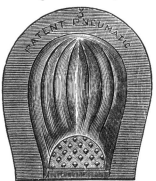

Fig 87.—Sheather's Pad.

One of the simplest anti-slipping pads is "Balls & Keep's Wedge-pad." It possesses one advantage in not covering up the whole under-surface of the foot. When properly fitted it is firmly retained and does its work, but a careless farrier may so apply it that it shifts on the foot. To fit it exactly the wall of the back part of the foot must be lowered more than that in front, so that shoe, foot and pad may all be closely adjusted.

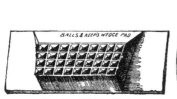

Fig. 88.—Wedge-Pad.

Fig. 89—Pad with Shoe attached.

What is called the "Bar-pad" is a leather plate on which an india-rubber pad occupies the whole of the back portion and it is fixed to the foot with a short shoe. This pad is not only an anti-slipping agent, it is anti-concussive, and for some diseases and some injuries of the heels is a most valuable appliance. For long-standing "corns," for cases of chronic laminitis, and for horses that markedly "go on their heels" the bar-pad is without doubt the most efficient arrangement yet invented. The best are made by Mr. Urquhart.

Fig. 90.—Bar-pad with Shoe.

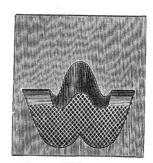

Fig. 91.—Without Shoe.

All these pads increase the cost of shoeing but what they save, by preventing falls and injuries to the horse and fear and anxiety to the driver, far more than balances the account in their favour. The cost however is an item, and inventors have turned their attention to the production of some other methods of applying rubber in connection with the shoe for the prevention of slipping.

Shoes have been manufactured into which cavities of different forms and sizes have been made. These are filled by correspondingly shaped pieces of rubber. The cavity must be so formed as to retain the rubber and this renders the manufacture very difficult except by the employment of malleable cast iron shoes. This is a great disadvantage.

Another plan is to make from rolled bar iron, a hollow shoe, section of which would be U-shaped but level to the foot. Into the groove so formed a thick cord of rubber is placed after the shoe is nailed on the foot. This wears well and affords good foot-hold but it entails the serious objection that the nails are difficult to drive and far from being so safe as in the ordinary shoe. If rubber is ever to be available in a grooved shoe it should be designed so that the nails and nail holes are not interfered with.

CHAPTER XI.

SHOEING COMPETITIONS.

The Agricultural Societies that have made Horse-shoeing
Competitions a feature of their Annual Shows have distinctly
done good to the art. In those districts which have had the
benefit of these competitions for many years past, horse-shoeing is best done. In those districts where no competitions
have been held shoeing is generally badly done. When the
farrier takes a pride in his work he is more careful with details. Provided proper principles are adopted, no calling is
more dependent upon care in details for the best results than
that of the farrier. Competitions stimulate emulation amongst
men. Public appreciation, as displayed by the prominence
given to the art by the Show authorities and by the admiring
crowd that generally assembles to see the men at work, en-
courages a feeling of responsibility and gratifies the natural
and honest pride of the workman. Very few trades have
suffered more from public neglect and indifference than that
of the farrier.

The success of a shoeing competition depends almost entirely upon the secretary of a show, unless that officer has
amongst his stewards an energetic horseman who has grasped
the importance of good shoeing and who possesses some
organising powers. In this connection I may perhaps offer
a word of acknowledgement for the work done by Mr. Clay,
to whose energy and skill the Royal Agricultural Society has
for many years been indebted for the success of its valuable
annual shoeing competition.

All the arrangements for the competition must be completed before the work is commenced, and upon their
perfection depends the success of the whole thing. There
should, if possible, be two classes—one for heavy horses
and one for light horses. At large competitions there
should also be a champion class. There are farriers who travel
from show to show and generally appear in the prize list.
This handicaps the local men, and is not encouraging to
those who have not quite risen to front rank. The object of
the competition is to improve the work of the district, and it
is quite a question whether the rules should not exclude men

who have taken, say, two first prizes at any large competition. The only argument in favour of letting the well known smith who has taken many prizes enter a competition is that his work may be seen, examined and imitated. By confining prize winners to the champion class this good would be attained; at the same time more encouragement would be given to local men.

The necessities for a competition include anvils, fires, tools, iron and horses.

For every five men there should be one anvil with its accompanying vice and forge. The anvil should be so placed that the sun is not full on the face of the workman. The exact relative position of anvil, vice and forge should be entrusted to a practical farrier, and the whole placed the night before they are wanted. Coal, nails and iron should also be provided. If competitors are allowed to bring their own iron or nails some poor man may be placed at a disadvantage, and the habitual competitor, versed in every detail, is given an advantage. Each man should bring all smaller tools he may want. In broken weather a canvas roof should be supplied both for horses and workmen. At all times a temporary wooden floor should be put down for the horses to stand upon. This should be a little longer than the line of anvils so that each man has his horse opposite his anvil. It should be at least twelve feet deep so that there is room enough behind and in front of the horses for men to pass. On the side farthest from the anvils a firm rail must be fixed to which the horses' halters may be tied, and outside of this—at least six feet distant—should be another line of post and rails to keep back spectators.

Horses have to be borrowed or hired, and one horse is sufficient for two competitors. Care should be taken not to have any horse with unusually bad feet. The most suitable horses are those with over-grown hoofs. Under no circumstances should a vicious or very fidgety horse be selected.

When time is not an object, the best test of a workman is to require him to make a fore and hind shoe and put them on the horse. At a one-day show, or at a competition when the entries are large, it is sufficient to require the making of a fore and hind shoe and the fitting and nailing on of the front one. A reasonable time should be fixed, and undue haste should be deprecated.

There should always be two judges, who should be supplied with books in which each division of the operation of shoeing should be separately marked. There are only three important divisions of the subject: (1) Preparation of the Foot, (2) Making the Shoes, and (3) Fitting and nailing on.

Sometimes these operations are marked separately for fore and hind feet. I consider this quite unnecessary. There is not sufficient difference either in principle or detail to require each foot to be specially marked. The judge of course notes every thing in his mind, and it is sufficient for him to estimate and mark the value of the work under the three different operations. The great fault I find with most competitions is that "the preparation" of the foot for the shoe is not more strictly defined. The competitors are permitted to mix up the "preparation" and the "fitting." Some of them do nothing to the foot until they commence to fit the shoe This is wrong, and every foot should be properly prepared—the bearing-surface formed and the proportions of the hoof attended to—before the fitting is attempted. A rule to this effect should be added to the conditions in the schedule of the competition. Each judge may perhaps be permitted to fix his own standard of marking but a uniform system would be useful for comparison. If the maximum be indicated by too small a figure difficulty often arises in exactly determining the merits of men who have come out equal in the totals, and there is too often, in a large class, a number whose marks are about equal. The three operations—preparing the foot, making the shoe, fitting and nailing on—are about equal in value. A maximum of five points in each is too small a number to make distinctive marking easy, but there is nothing gained by adopting a higher maximum than ten. A marking sheet for the judges of a shoeing-competition may be something in this form :

CLASS ——

No. of Competitor.	Preparation of Foot.	Making Shoe.	Fitting and Nailing on.	Total.	Remarks.

The stewards should see that each competitor has a number, and that the same number is attached to the side of the horse on which he works. The steward also should take the time at which each batch of competitors commence and see that none exceed it.

Excessive rasping of shoes should be prohibited, and the men should see the sizes and kinds of nails provided that they may make their "fuller" and nail holes accordingly.

Shoeing competitions are almost entirely confined to country districts. It is a great pity that they are not attempted in large towns. The only difficulty is the expense. It would well repay large horse-owners to subscribe and support this method of improving the art.

In conclusion I must say that the best of all ways to improve the art is by giving practical instruction at the anvil. A few lessons from a competent practical teacher are worth more than all books or lectures, as the work has then to be done, errors are pointed out and corrected, and reasons given for each step as it is attempted.

The Berkshire County Council has adopted a travelling forge —the suggestion of Mr. Albert Wheatley, V.S., of Reading— which is accompanied by an instructor and passes from town to town and village to village. In this way is supplied the tuition which used to be obtained by apprenticeship to a good workman. Other County Councils should adopt this method.

THE END.

INDEX.

———o———

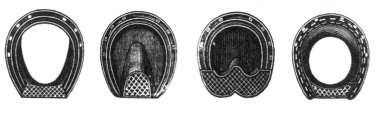

GET THE LATEST INFORMATION ON HOOF CARE!

With knowledge being your most important tool, *American Farriers Journal*, the "hands-on" magazine for professional farriers around the world, offers a wide variety of valuable hoof-care information through our magazine, books, special reports, DVDs, product sets and educational events.